# CHICAGO GREAT WESTERN
## In Color

CGW #115C with freight leaving St. Paul. (Ed Kanak)

## Lloyd E. Stagner

Copyright © 1997 Morning Sun Books, Inc.
**All rights reserved.** This book may not be reproduced in part or in whole without written permission from the publisher, except in the case of brief quotations or reproductions of the cover for the purposes of review.

Published by
**Morning Sun Books, Inc.**
9 Pheasant Lane
Scotch Plains, NJ 07076

Library of Congress
Catalog Card No. 96-078485

First Printing
ISBN 1-878887-67-X

Color separation and printing by
**The Kutztown Publishing Co., Inc.**
Kutztown, Pennsylvania

### Dedication
In memory of Jim Buckley, Jim Konas and Roger Puta.

### Acknowledgements
My sincere appreciation to all the photographers who were lineside in the 1950s and 60s to capture the CGW spirit displayed in this book. A special note to Randy Garnhart, Mark and Mike Nelson for their technical input.

| | | |
|---|---|---|
| THE ROSTER ............................ 7 | Byron ..................................... 41 | McINTIRE DISTRICT ................. 89 |
| CHICAGO ................................ 12 | German Valley ....................... 42 | Rochester ............................. 92 |
| CHICAGO DISTRICT ................. 19 | South Freeport ...................... 43 | Simpson ............................... 95 |
|   Forest Park ........................ 19 | Pearl City ............................... 44 | Stewartville .......................... 97 |
|   Maywood ........................... 21 | Stockton ................................ 44 | Racine .................................. 97 |
|   Bellwood ........................... 22 | Winston Tunnel ..................... 47 | TWIN CITIES ........................... 98 |
|   Elmhurst ........................... 22 | Portage ................................. 52 | ST. PAUL DISTRICT ................ 105 |
|   Villa Park .......................... 26 | East Dubuque ....................... 54 | Randolph ........................... 105 |
|   Lombard ........................... 27 | Dubuque ............................... 55 | Kenyon .............................. 106 |
|   Dean Road ........................ 28 | Fairground ............................ 57 | Dodge Center .................... 108 |
|   Gretna ............................... 29 | Durango ................................ 58 | Hayfield ............................. 109 |
|   Ingalton ............................ 30 | OELWEIN ................................ 60 | New Hampton .................... 113 |
|   St. Charles ....................... 32 | COUNCIL BLUFFS-OMAHA ....... 74 | Fredricksburg .................... 113 |
|   Virgil ................................. 36 |   Council Bluffs ..................... 74 | DES MOINES & |
|   Richardson ....................... 36 | MASON CITY DISTRICT ........... 83 | KANSAS CITY DISTRICTS ....... 114 |
|   Sycamore ......................... 37 |   Austin .................................. 83 | Fairbank ............................ 114 |
|   Clare ................................. 38 |   Mason City .......................... 85 | Waterloo ............................ 115 |
|   Esmond ............................ 38 |   Clear Lake Juction ............. 85 | Des Moines ....................... 118 |
|   Stillman Valley ................. 39 | MANKOTA DISTRICT ................ 86 | St. Joseph ......................... 121 |
|   Holcomb ........................... 40 | WINONA BRANCH .................... 87 | KANSAS CITY ........................ 122 |

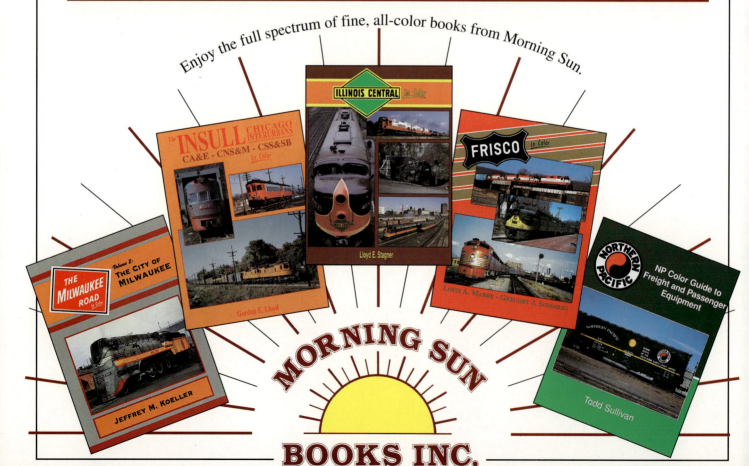

# CHICAGO GREAT WESTERN In Color

Chicago Great Western Railway Company was organized in January 1892, with railroad magnate A.B. Stickney's consolidation of his Minnesota and Northwestern with his Chicago, St. Paul & Kansas City. Stickney had pushed the M&NW into Chicago, via Dubuque in 1888, and the CStP&KC was in Leavenworth KS in 1891 where trackage rights were obtained over the Missouri Pacific to Kansas City. CGW bought the Mason City & Fort Dodge and constructed trackage to Council Bluffs in 1903, rounding out the system in the geographical area that it remained for the next 65 years. Although CGW routes between its principal terminals were longer, it competed with railroads with shorter mileage on passenger traffic and soon was running twelve named trains, including the crack GREAT WESTERN LIMITED between Chicago and the Twin Cities. Serving Rochester MN, home of the famed Mayo clinic helped CGW to be a strong factor in traffic to and from that point. Stickney's early ambition was to make the CGW the "Pennsylvania Lines of the West". Perhaps, an overly ambitious dream, CGW was a respected competitor although it had longer mileage between all the important terminals. "The Corn Belt Route" survived the panic of 1907 by taking bankruptcy, and upon leaving court protection it entered the fold of J.P. Morgan and Company who appointed Samuel M. Felton, a talented railroad man as President.

Great Western prospered during the 1920s, but in 1929, fell under the control of the Bremo Corporation, and Patrick B. Joyce who proceeded to loot the company. Deferred maintenance was general and the effects of the Great Depression on traffic levels brought about another bankruptcy in 1935, which lasted until 1941. The vast traffic of World War II brought a return to reasonable prosperity. "The Corn Belt Route" was controlled by the so-called "Kansas City Group" commencing in 1948, and William M. Deramus III, the 33 year old son of the President of the Kansas City Southern was elected President. The youngest President of a Class I railroad proceeded to shake up the company with a consolidation of departments, personnel and facilities. Some short branch lines were abandoned and much of the passenger service discontinued. Long 150 to 250 car freight trains, pulled by six or seven "F" units became the norm on through freight trains. This was at a time when most railroads used a maximum of four units, or 6000 h.p. Mr. Deramus left the CGW for the Katy in January 1957, but his hand picked successor E.T. Reidy continued the Deramus operating philosophy.

As the early merger movement gained momentum in the 1960s, CGW attempted to align itself with several railroads, including the Rock Island, Soo Line and a three way combination of CGW, Katy and Chicago & Eastern Illinois. None of these proposals bore fruit, and on November 13, 1964, CGW and the Chicago & North Western filed a merger application with the Interstate Commerce Commission. The application was not approved until April 20, 1967 and legal challenges by the Soo Line, delayed the effective date until July 1, 1968. Although traffic increased on the Kansas City line after the merger, most other routes fell into disuse and were abandoned. The Kansas City line followed when the Rock Island was liquidated in 1980, and C&NW acquired the shorter "Spine Line" from the Twin Cities to Kansas City.

*(Above)* After using the so-called Maple Leaf emblem, CGW adopted the Corn Belt Route slogan about 1910.
*(Randy Garnhart)*

*(Below)* CGW 113A and friends at Minneapolis, August 23, 1969. *(Gordon E. Lloyd)*

*(W.L. Heitter)*

Chicago Great Western was somewhat of a railroad industry innovator dating from its 1910 use of gasoline-electric motor cars, and the acquisition the same year of ten 2-6-6-2 Mallets. Some 4-6-2 Pacifics were painted red, and a couple had a semi-streamlined English appearance. Thirty-six big 2-10-4s were built by Baldwin and Lima in 1930-1931 for service between Chicago-Oelwien-South St. Paul, also Oelwien to East Leavenworth, where bridge restrictions on the Missouri River prevented their operation through to Kansas City.

Famous railroader John W. Barriger dubbed the CGW "A mountain railroad in prairie territory." The 2-10-4s and later six unit 6000 h.p. diesels were well suited for this type of operation.

In 1936, Great Western became the first "steam road" to embrace permanent "piggyback" service, a lasting innovation, whereas its earlier famous passenger service, all disappeared on September 30, 1965.

Diesel-electric motive power came fast, commencing in 1947. Steam operations ended in early 1950 and all steam power was retired by August. During that year, only 13,381 of nearly two million freight locomotive miles were performed with steam power, plus an insignificant 52 miles of passenger train service, and 2262 miles of yard service.

Some CGW statistics for 1959: Equipment owned included 141 diesel and one other locomotive units, 5,496 freight cars, 34 passenger cars including one motor car, and 142 miscellaneous cars. Of the freight tonnage 45% was originated and 55% received from connections. Surprisingly, the most important item was lumber which totaled 21,030 cars, all received from connections at the Twin Cities and Council Bluffs. Corn, wheat and other farm products aggregated slightly more than lumber at 21,832 cars of diversified tonnage. 10,657 carloads of canned food were handled, plus 7,061 cars of fresh meat. Coal handled, much from connections, totaled 8,045 cars, iron and steel 6,064 cars and petroleum products 4,174. So, CGW had a diversified tonnage base. By 1959, only 21,938 passengers boarded CGW passenger trains, which by then had been reduced to Omaha-Minneapolis, and Kansas City-Minneapolis service, the latter trains running six days a week. Readers interested in the complete history of the Chicago Great Western are referred to H. Roger Grant's *The Corn Belt Route*, Northern Illinois University Press, DeKalb IL. 1984.

In *Chicago Great Western In Color*, we will take a colorful look at the last years of the "Corn Belt Route," or the "Great Weedy" as it was sometimes irreverently referred to. An important cog in the nation's rail system for over three-quarters of a century.

*(Above)* A Corn Belt Route emblem as painted on the depot at West Concord, MN in June 1970, almost two years after the CGW-C&NW merger. *(Randy Garnhart)*

CGW 36, Chicago, October 3, 1964.
*(K.C. Henkels, R.J. Yanosey collection)*

CGW 206, Chicago, October 27, 1964.
*(K.C. Henkels, R.J. Yanosey collection)*

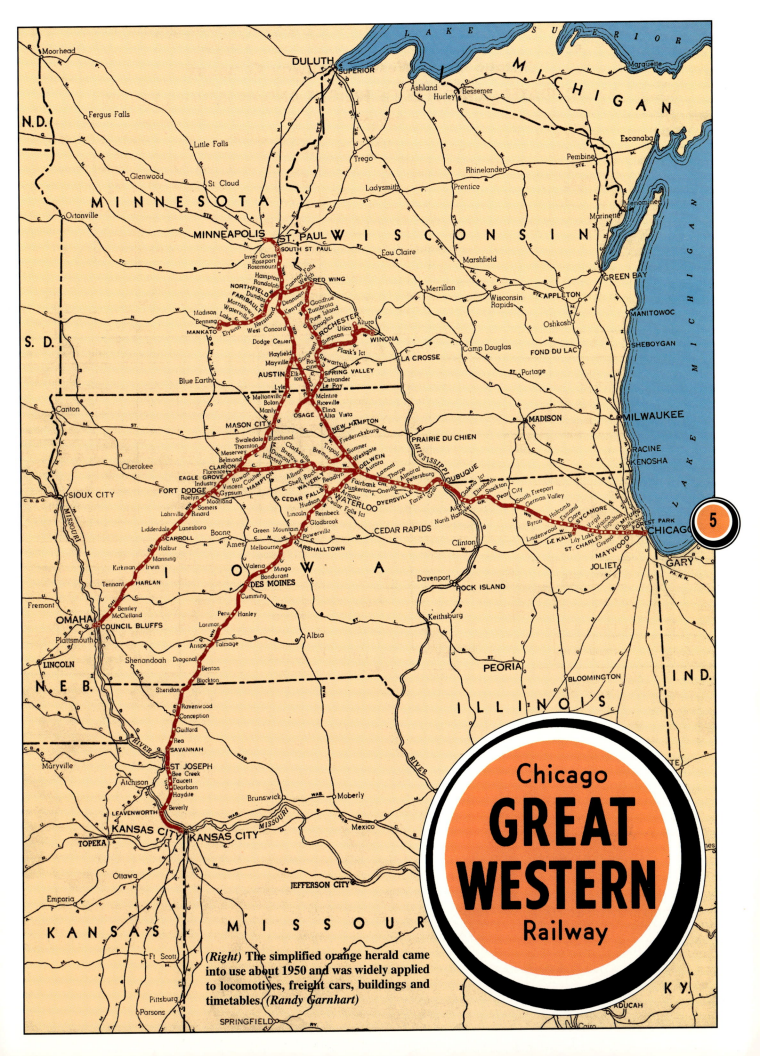

*(Right)* The simplified orange herald came into use about 1950 and was widely applied to locomotives, freight cars, buildings and timetables. *(Randy Garnhart)*

The basic building block of CGW road freight locomotives, the EMD F-unit. CGW FP7 116A was at Chicago, May 19, 1967.
*(K.C. Henkels, R.J. Yanosey collection)*

# CHICAGO GREAT WESTERN
## DIESEL LOCOMOTIVES

| Eng. Nos. | Builder | Model | H.P. | Years Built | Notes |
|---|---|---|---|---|---|
| 1 | Baldwin | | 175 | 1925 | Gas Mechanical loco scrapped 1956 |
| 2-4 | Westinghouse | | 800 | 1934-35 | |
| 5-7 | E.M.C. | SC | 600 | 1936 | |
| 8-10 | Alco-G.E. | S2 | 1000 | 1947 | |
| 11-15 | Alco-G.E. | S1 | 660 | 1948 | |
| 16-31 | E.M.D. | NW2 | 1000 | 1948-49 | |
| 32-41 | Baldwin | DS4-4-1000 | 1000 | 1949 | |
| 50-57 | Alco G.E. | RS2 | 1500 | 1949 | |
| 58AB-66AB | E.M.D. | TR2 | 2000 | 1949 | "Cow and calf" |
| 120-121 | E.M.D. | GP7 | 1500 | 1951 | #120 rebuilt as GP9R in 1956 |
| 101AC-115AC | E.M.D. | F3A | 1500 | 1947-49 | Trade in 1963 on GP30s (6) Trade in 1966 on SD40s (6) |
| 101B-112B | E.M.D. | F3B | 1500 | 1947-49 | Trade in 1966 on SD40s (5) |
| 101D-104D | E.M.D. | F3B | 1500 | 1949 | Trade in 1966 on SD40 (1) |
| 116AC | E.M.D. | FP7 | 1500 | 1950 | |
| 150-152 | E.M.D. | F3A | 1500 | 1948-49 | Equipped for passenger service Trade in 1963 on GP30 (1) |
| 153-156 | E.M.D. | F7A | 1500 | 1949 | Trade in 1963 on GP30 (1) |
| 105D-110D | E.M.D. | F7B | 1500 | 1949 | Trade in 1966 on SD40 (1) |
| 112D-116D | E.M.D. | F7B | 1500 | 1949-51 | |
| 113B-116B | E.M.D. | F7B | 1500 | 1949-50 | |
| 116EFG | E.M.D. | F7B | 1500 | 1951 | |
| 201-208 | E.M.D. | GP30 | 2250 | 1963 | |
| 401-409 | E.M.D. | SD40 | 3000 | 1966 | |

# THE ROSTER

*(Above)* Alco GE S2 No. 9, CGW Class D-3, was assigned to yard service in Chicago on April 2, 1961. Built in May 1947, the nine "spot" became C&NW 1014 after the 1968 merger. *(G.E. Lloyd)*

*(Above)* Another Alco-GE S2 1000 h.p. switching locomotive was working at Chicago, on April 2, 1961. Numbers 8-9-10 were all built in 1947 and would make it to the C&NW merger. *(G.E. Lloyd)*

*(Above)* A set of six Fs with F3A 115C in the lead was on hand at the Chicago Transfer engine terminal on August 20, 1961. They would depart for Oelwein on Manifest train No. 91, due out at 11:00 p.m. *(Bill Volkmer collection)*

*(Right)* CGW 35 was in the simplified scheme when photographed at Cicero, IL on March 7, 1965. The 1000hp Baldwins were sixteen years old by that date and still carried their as-built prime movers, unlike their C&NW brethren.
*(C.H. Zeiler)*

*(Above)* SW7s 20 and 24, built by EMD in May 1948, and Baldwin DS4-4-1000 No. 38 were among the switch power assigned to the Chicago Transfer yard on May 2, 1963. No. 20 still sported its 1948 EMD-created paint scheme. *(R.E. Puta, M. Finzer collection)*

*(Right)* On February 21, 1965, No. 143 was handled with Fs 104A-105B-106C-116F-110D-112C with 77 cars, on B&OCT trackage near Oak Park. *(J.J. Buckley)*

*(Right)* GP7 121, still sporting its September 1951 applied paint, was awaiting a call at the Chicago Transfer engine terminal on October 3, 1964. The 120-121 were used on the Sycamore Turn and the Stockton Turn.
*(G.E. Lloyd)*

*(Above)* No. 143 was out of Chicago Transfer and on the doubletrack B&OCT, behind GP30s 201-203-202-204 pulling 29 cars, on February 14, 1965. The manifest would pick up additional tonnage at Bellwood off the Indiana Harbor Belt. *(J.J. Buckley)*

*(Right)* A general view of the diesel house at Chicago Transfer on February 21, 1965 with Baldwin DS4-4-1000 No. 36 and another yard unit and some road units, also on hand.
*(J.J. Buckley)*

*(Left)* Baldwin DS4-4-1000 switchers 40 and 39, also two Alco S2s were on hand at the Chicago Transfer diesel house on August 20, 1966. Diesel switchers owned by CGW included ten Baldwin, eight Alco, seventeen EMDs, three EMC and three Westinghouse units. *(C.H. Zeiler)*

*(Above and below)* The clear, autumn afternoon of October 31, 1965 found a six unit set of F "covered wagons" on hand, with 104A and 113A on the operating ends. This set arrived at Chicago Transfer on No. 192 and would leave on No. 91 the following morning. *(C.H. Zeiler)*

*(Left)* GP30 205, which was built by Electro-Motive in 1963 at the start of the so-called "second generation of diesel locomotives" was outside the Chicago Transfer diesel house on November 29, 1965. It would be renumbered to 806 by the Chicago & North Western in 1968. *(J.J. Buckley)*

*(Below)* Manifest train 143 was preparing to leave Chicago Transfer on the first day of 1966 with F units 111C-112D-102D-115B-116A, which included all models of "covered wagons" owned by CGW.
*(J.J. Buckley)*

*(Right)* The final CGW diesel acquisitions were nine EMD SD40s acquired in 1966 two years before the merger. In this photo one year old #403 awaits a call to action on May 9, 1967 at Chicago. *(K.C. Henkels, R.J. Yanosey collection)*

# CHICAGO

As one of the last railroads to reach Chicago, in 1888, the Chicago Great Western did not enjoy a favorable terminal location. A small yard and engine house was established at Chicago Transfer, and trackage rights were obtained over the Baltimore & Ohio Chicago Terminal RR to CGW Jct. at Forest Park, three miles west of Chicago Transfer. Passenger trains ran over the B&OCT to the Grand Central Station, which was shared with the Baltimore & Ohio, Pere Marquette and Soo Line. Passenger locomotives were handled at the B&OCT roundhouse at Robey Street. Most interchange was carried out at Bellwood, 5.8 miles west of Chicago Transfer, with the Indiana Harbor Belt which allowed the CGW to interchange traffic with 26 other railroads in 1957. By 1968, the number of interchange railroads had decreased to 20 due to various mergers. In October 1964 an average of 110 cars were interchanged with the IHB each day. In 1956, the Bellwood station was open 24 hours per day and manned with an agent, six clerks and two operators. There was a minimal amount of local industry on the CGW in Chicago, but most industries in the Chicago switching district were open to reciprocal switching, allowing the Great Western to secure carload traffic, both originating and terminating. Until less-than-carload service was discontinued in the 1960s, CGW maintained a freight house on B&OCT trackage, near the Chicago "Loop" and dispatched yard engines to switch the freight house in the morning and again in the evening, when merchandise cars were brought to Chicago Transfer for movement on No. 53; later No. 91. For many years general offices were located at 309 West Jackson, in the "Loop" but in the 1950s, the Operating Department was shifted to Oelwein, the executive, treasury and industrial development departments were moved to Kansas City, leaving only traffic department officers in the "Railroad Capital of the World."

*(Right)* A mixture of GP30s 206, 205, 202 F7B 107D and F3B 101D prepared to leave Chicago Transfer on No. 143 on October 2, 1966. *(J. Piersen)*

*(Below)* Manifest No. 143 was rolling west on the doubletrack B&OCT on November 6, 1966 with SD40s 404-405 and Fs 106D-116E-113D moving 23 cars to Oelwein.
*(J.J. Buckley)*

*(Above)* Grimy SD40s 401, 409, 408 are in charge of #143 on B&OCT trackage in Chicago on November 13, 1966. The order for nine SD40s was received earlier in 1966. They were the first (and only) six-motor diesels purchased by CGW.
*(J.J. Buckley)*

*(Below)* Near Austin Avenue on the B&OCT, #143 was handled by seven F units, with 1949 built F3A 114C in control on a snowy January 5, 1967, a month that would see Chicago railroad operations paralyzed by a record blizzard. *(J. Piersen)*

*(Above)* Baldwin switcher 41 was pulling a transfer cut near Oak Park on B&OCT trackage that included another switcher, a caboose, wrecker derrick and a cut of freight cars on March 22, 1967. The adjacent forty-foot boxcars would soon be as technologically obsolete as the Baldwin. *(J. Piersen)*

*(Below)* The Chicago Great Western "trademark" locomotive—six or more F-units lashed up to produce a gargantuan 9000 hp. No wonder that the thought of just three SD40s appealed to the accountants. F units 108C, 116G, 110B, 114B, 106D, 114A were arriving at the Chicago Transfer yard on an eastbound train on May 6, 1967. A Chicago Transit Authority station is in the right background. *(J. Piersen)*

*(Above)* Along Austin Avenue on B&OCT trackage, Fs 115A, 116B, 106B, 116D, 108B and 111A roll a short #143 train on June 10, 1967. *(J. Piersen)*

*(Right)* Alco S2 engine 8 looks good at Chicago Transfer on June 11, 1967. No. 8 was the first S2 built for the CGW in February 1947 and was renumbered to C&NW 1010 in 1968. The S2 developed 1000 h.p. and weighed 115 tons in working order. *(Bill Volkmer)*

*(Below)* With a summer thunderstorm in the distance GP30 205 and three companions wait a call at Chicago Transfer on June 11, 1967. CGW had the unit's roofs painted black which had the effect of making their GP30's sculpted brake blister less pronounced. *(Bill Volkmer)*

*(Above)* A night view of the Chicago Transfer engine facility and TOFC area on the evening of June 18, 1967. *(J. Piersen)*

*(Below)* Baldwin DS4-4-1000 No. 41 was still in its 1949 delivered paint scheme at Chicago Transfer yard in the twilight of its life on September 10, 1967. These Baldwin yard engines weighed 235,000 pounds, and developed 58,750 pounds of starting tractive effort. *(R.E. Puta, M. Finzer collection)*

*(Above)* The power on #143 of September 10, 1967, near Harlem Avenue in Oak Park included FP7 116, F7Bs 116G and 114B, F3B 101B and GP30 201. The "tell tales" over the B&OCT tracks indicate an overhead obstruction is close. *(J. Piersen)*

*(Below)* November 19, 1967 found Jim Buckley on the CGW to again photograph #143 on the B&OCT west of Chicago Transfer with "covered wagons" 112C, 108B, 103D, 102B, 107C in charge of a 52-car train. *(J.J. Buckley)*

*(Above)* A little while later, on November 19, 1967, Buckley caught No. 192 arriving with GP30s 204, 207, 205 and 201 pulling 54 cars that included two Armour & Company meat "reefers head out." *(J.J. Buckley)*

*(Left)* At the Chicago Transfer engine house, on November 19, 1967, photographer Buckley found 19 year old NW2 switcher 17. The wings and paint scheme were straight out of EMD's design department. *(J.J. Buckley)*

*(Below)* We complete our color photo coverage of the Chicago terminal of the Chicago Great Western with Baldwin DS4-4-1000 engine 41 in the final switcher paint scheme on November 25, 1967. Built in 1949, it would be the last Baldwin product purchased by CGW. *(J.J. Buckley)*

# CHICAGO DISTRICT

The 245.8 miles of the Chicago District, Eastern Division of the Chicago Great Western, which extended from Chicago Transfer to Oelwein, enjoyed the heaviest ton miles on the railway. The westbound ruling grade was 1.1%, with one percent prevailing eastbound. In the steam era, the Texas type (2-10-4) Class T-1, T-2 and T-3 locomotives were limited to 2900 tons. Three westbound manifest trains were carded, Nos. 51, 53, 55, with eastbound manifests numbered 50, 52, 54 and 58. Extra trains increased traffic to an average of six through freights in each direction. Dieselization with multi-unit F type EMD locomotives resulted in the schedules being reduced to Nos. 91 and 143 westbound and Nos. 90 and 192 eastbound. Some local freight service operated on a turn-around basis from several intermediate points. Passenger service on the Chicago District included the 4-6-2 powered MINNESOTAN between Chicago-Twin Cities until May 10, 1949. Motor trains 3-4 continued to operate providing local service, however in 1950, Nos. 7-8 were established with a single F unit, with steam generator, a baggage-RPO car, baggage car and coach. These trains provided the only CGW passenger service to the Windy City, until their discontinuance between Chicago and Dubuque August 11, 1956. The Dubuque-Oelwein portion lasted until September 29, 1956.

CGW passenger trains used Grand Central Station in Chicago, operating over the Baltimore & Ohio Chicago Terminal. Engine facilities and a small yard were maintained at Chicago Transfer. Most freight was interchanged with the Indiana Harbor Belt at Bellwood. Principal freight moving east on the Chicago District included meat and other packing house products, grain products, lumber and some livestock although the stock traffic disappeared by the early 1960s. Westbound tonnage was mostly merchandise and manufactured goods. TOFC or "piggyback" had replaced much of the boxcar merchandise business by the 1960s. The most salient physical feature of the Chicago District was the half mile long Winston tunnel, at Mile Post 152.4, about three miles east of Aiken which was opened in 1887. CGW also used the Illinois Central tunnel at East Dubuque. Most grades were of the momentum type, however there was 8.1 mile helper district between Graf and Farley in the steam era. There was a wye at Farley for turning helpers. Some of the first welded rail used in the United States was installed in 1939 between Mileposts 213 and 214. The high cost of installation made further additional welded rail not feasible until better methods were developed in the 1950s, however the 1939 project was another CGW innovation.

## FOREST PARK

*(Below)* At Forest Park, 10.3 miles from the Chicago Grand Central Station, No. 3 was westbound on June 17, 1950 with "doodlebug" 1009 pulling the usual baggage car and heavy weight coach. RPO service was provided with a mail sorting section in the motor car, a noisy work place for the RPO clerk. *(J.J. Buckley)*

*(Above)* On May 31, 1950 motor 1009 hauling local passenger train No. 3 passed over the Des Plaines River bridge near Forest Park. Oelwein is 235.3 miles away. *(J.J. Buckley)*

*(Below)* GP30s 201-207-202-205 had westbound manifest No. 143 rolling over the Fox River bridge near St. Charles on the afternoon of September 11, 1966. By this late date in CGW history, GP30s and SD40s had replaced multi-unit F-consists on some Chicago District trains. *(J. Piersen)*

 ## MAYWOOD

*(Above)* No. 143 of June 15, 1967 was powered by Fs 116C-102B-111A-113D-101D-116A as it passed the station at Maywood IL, 4.3 miles from the Chicago Transfer yard. Looks like a virtual "wall" of F-units! *(J. Piersen)*

*(Below)* Manifest train No. 143 was close to on time when it passed Maywood on the afternoon of November 19, 1967 powered by Fs 112C-108B-103D-102B-109C-152. *(J.J. Buckley)*

## BELLWOOD

*(Above)* F3A 106C headed a five-unit consist of Fs in the original paint scheme westbound near Bellwood on October 8, 1950. *(G.E. Lloyd)*

## ELMHURST

*(Right)* A cold day in February 1967 found time freight #143 rolling west with three SD40s at Poplar Avenue in Elmhurst, a Chicago suburban community that enjoyed suburban service provided by the Chicago & North Western. *(T.E. Hoffman)*

*(Below)* In the last winter of CGW operations manifest No. 192 was near Elmhurst with F3A 107C and four other Fs hauling 70 cars on December 3, 1967. The Indiana Harbor Belt meat is on the head end to be set out at Bellwood, only 3.7 miles from Elmhurst. *(J.J. Buckley)*

*(Below)* Bay window caboose 632 brings up the markers on the rear of No. 192 at Elmhurst on December 3, 1967. *(J.J. Buckley)*

 *(Above)* Alco-GE S2 switcher 9 was tied up in front of the Elmhurst depot between switching chores on December 28, 1962, while the crew receives further instructions from the local freight agent.

*(Below)* Station work complete, the Alco waffs out a little black smoke as the local gets underway. Double track extended from Chicago to Elmhurst.

Another view of the Chicago District way freight with Alco GE S2 switcher 9, crossing the Salt Creek bridge in Elmhurst on December 28, 1962.
*(All, R.E. Puta, M. Finzer collection)*

*(Above)* On a clear April 20, 1962 time freight No. 143 banged over the Illinois Central Iowa Division main line at Elmhurst. FP7 116, one of the last two F-type units purchased by CGW (in 1950), is in control.

*(R.E. Puta, M. Finzer collection)*

## VILLA PARK

*(Below)* Villa Park was a non-agency station located 1.5 miles west of the Illinois Central crossing at Elmhurst. An eastbound train with F3A 110A and a Geep has stopped to set out some cars in January 1968.

*(T. Hoffman collection)*

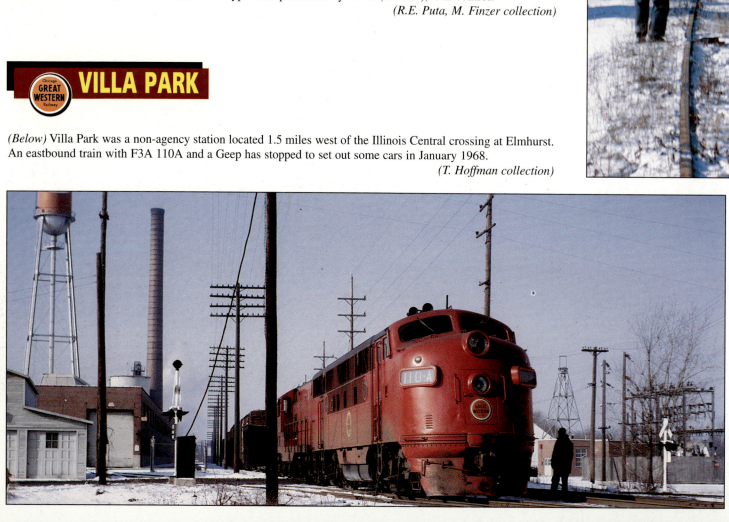

 **LOMBARD**

*(Above)* On December 28, 1962, the way freight with S2 engine 9 took siding at Lombard for manifest train 192, with the usual six F unit locomotive consist.

*(R.E. Puta, M. Finzer collection)*

*(Right)* Way freight, Extra 9 West continues west with its short train near Lombard, 4.5 miles west of Elmhurst, also on December 28, 1962. The 1947-built #9 was fifteen years old by then, but still capable of performing these "road-switcher" duties.

*(R.E. Puta, M. Finzer collection)*

## DEAN ROAD

*(Below)* Two months before the end of the Chicago Great Western, No. 192, passed Dean Road, with three SD40s, with engine 406 on the "point." Meat "reefers" behind one boxcar will be set out at Bellwood for movement east via the Indiana Harbor Belt.
*(Jim Konas, J.J. Buckley collection)*

 **GRETNA**

*(Above)* Automatic block signals and a short stretch of centralized traffic control guarded the entire Chicago-Oelwein mileage of the Chicago District. The small depot at Gretna, 25.6 miles from Chicago, was equipped with an electric color light train order signal. *(R. E. Puta)*

*(Left)* One of only two GP7s rostered by the CGW, the 1951 built #121 was operating long hood forward while on a way freight train at Gretna on August 14, 1962.
*(R.E. Puta, M. Finzer collection)*

## INGALTON

*(Above)* On the Fourth of July 1962, No. 143 passed Ingalton, 30.7 miles west of Chicago in charge of F3A 115A and five unidentified F units. No. 143 was due out of Chicago Transfer at 12 noon and due at Ingalton at 1:30 p.m. and due into Oelwein at 11 p.m. *(R.E. Puta, M. Finzer collection)*

*(Above)* During the last winter of CGW's life, on January 5, 1968, manifest train No. 192 led by FP7 116C passed the Ingalton station building. *(R.E. Puta, M. Finzer collection)*

*(Below)* Great Western's other GP7 #120 was rebuilt in January 1956 by EMD into a 1500 hp GP9m. At Ingalton, the 120 was on hand with a caboose to protect way freight service on March 23, 1966. *(C.H. Zeiler)*

 **ST. CHARLES**

*(Above)* The inverted through truss span bridge over the Fox River near St. Charles offered a stunning photo location to photograph Train 4, with Motor car 1009 on June 3, 1950. *(J.J. Buckley)*

### Chicago, Dubuque—to Clarion, Fort Dodge, Omaha

For complete local schedules Chicago to Oelwein, see Table 2.

| Read Down | | | | | Read Up | |
|---|---|---|---|---|---|---|
| 1 DAILY | 3-35-31 MOTOR | Mls | TABLE 6 | 32-36-2 MOTOR | 4 EXS MOT | |
| | | | Central Time (Grand Cent. Sta.) | | | |
| PM | PM | | | AM | | |
| 6 45 | ‡11 00 | 0 | Lv....Chicago......Ar | * 8 50 | †7 | |
| 7 06 | 11 25 | 10 | Lv....Forest Park....Ar | 8 23 | 7 | |
| 7 45 | 12 16 | 36 | Lv.....St. Charles.....Ar | 7 45 | 6 | |
| 8 25 | 1 01 | 57 | Lv......Sycamore......Ar | 7 15 | 5 | |
| 11 25 | 4 51 | 172 | Lv......Dubuque......Ar | 4 15 | 2 | |
| 1 45 | 7 30 | 246 | Ar.Oelwein 1, 2, 5..Lv | * 2 15 | 11 | |
| AM | † 9 00 | 246 | Lv.....Oelwein......Ar | † 6 15 | P | |
| | 9 18 | 255 | Lv.......Oran.......Ar | 5 51 | | |
| | 9 31 | 262 | Lv.....Readlyn.....Ar | 5 38 | | |
| From Minneapolis, See Table 4. | f 9 44 | 269 | Lv...Denver Jct....Ar | f 5 25 | Runs to Minneap's., | |
| | 10 00 | 275 | Lv.....Waverly.....Ar | 5 15 | | |
| | 10 12 | 282 | Lv...Shell Rock....Ar | 5 01 | MOTOR | |
| | 10 25 | 288 | Lv...Clarksville....Ar | 4 47 | | |
| | 10 40 | 295 | Lv......Allison......Ar | 4 34 | | |
| | 10 50 | 301 | Lv......Bristow......Ar | 4 22 | | |
| | 10 58 | 305 | Lv......Dumont......Ar | 4 14 | | |
| | 11 11 | 312 | Lv......Hansell......Ar | 4 02 | | |
| | 11 25 | 317 | Lv..Hampton, Iowa..Ar | 3 52 | | |
| | 11 41 | 326 | Lv......Coulter......Ar | 3 36 | | |
| | 11 58 | 335 | Lv......Rowan......Ar | 3 20 | | |
| 33 | f12 04 | 338 | Lv......Solberg......Ar | f 3 12 | 3 | |
| DAILY | †12 15 | 345 | Ar.....Clarion 4.....Lv | † 3 00 | DAI | |
| 1 58 | * 2 40 | 345 | Lv......Clarion......Ar | * 1 05 | 1 | |
| .l.. | | 350 | Ar.....Florence.....Lv | | .o | |
| 2 13 | 3 00 | 354 | Ar....Eagle Grove....Lv | 12 38 | 1 | |
| .l.. | ..k.. | 359 | Ar.......Nuel.......Lv | ..k.. | .o | |
| .l.. | | 363 | Ar......Vincent......Lv | 12 25 | .o | |
| .l.. | ..k.. | 367 | Ar......Industry......Lv | ..k.. | .o | |
| 2 55 | 3 45 | 373 | Ar....Fort Dodge....Lv | 12 05 | 12 | |
| .l.. | f4 02 | 380 | Ar.....Moorland.....Lv | 11 32 | .o | |
| .l.. | ..k.. | 384 | Ar......Roelyn......Lv | ..k.. | .o | |
| .l.. | 4 14 | 389 | Ar......Somers......Lv | 11 21 | .o | |
| .l.. | f4 20 | 393 | Ar......Rinard......Lv | 11 16 | .o | |
| 3 42 | 4 29 | 399 | Ar.....Lohrville.....Lv | 11 08 | .o | |
| .l.. | ..k.. | 403 | Ar.....Wightman.....Lv | ..k.. | .o | |
| .l.. | 4 43 | 408 | Ar.....Lanesboro.....Lv | 10 54 | .o | |
| .l.. | 4 52 | 414 | Ar.....Lidderdale.....Lv | 10 45 | .o | |
| 4 20 | 5 05 | 421 | Ar......Carroll......Lv | 10 35 | 11 | |
| .l.. | | 429 | Ar......Halbur......Lv | 10 16 | .o | |
| ..l-u.. | 5 32 | 438 | Ar.....Manning.....Lv | 10 05 | 11 | |
| .l.. | | 443 | Ar......Botna......Lv | f 9 54 | .o | |
| .l.. | 5 41 | 449 | Ar.......Irwin.......Lv | 9 46 | .o | |
| .l.. | 5 51 | 455 | Ar......Kirkman......Lv | f 9 38 | .o | |
| 5 24 | 6 11 | 461 | Ar......Harlan......Lv | 9 30 | 10 | |
| .l.. | ..k.. | 469 | Ar......Tennant......Lv | 9 13 | .o | |
| .l.. | ..k.. | 476 | Ar......Magill......Lv | ..k.. | .o | |
| .l.. | ..k.. | 480 | Ar......Minden......Lv | ..k.. | .o | |
| .l.. | ..k.. | 487 | Ar......Bentley......Lv | 8 47 | .o | |
| .l.. | ..k.. | 492 | Ar.....McClelland.....Lv | 8 40 | .o | |
| .l.. | ..k.. | 497 | Ar......Gilliat......Lv | ..k.. | .o | |
| 6 30 | 7 24 | 505 | Ar...Council Bluffs...Lv | 8 20 | 9 | |
| 7 10 | * 8 00 | 509 | Ar.......Omaha.......Lv | * 8 00 | 8 | |
| AM | PM | | (Burlington Sta.) | AM | P | |

*(Left)* A typical CGW depot of frame construction painted tuscan red with cream trim is modeled by St. Charles on June 23, 1962. This Illinois city was also served by the Chicago & North Western and by the interurban Chicago, Aurora & Elgin.

*(R.E. Puta, M. Finzer collection)*

*(Above and below)* Two views, head end and rear end of manifest train No. 143 crossing the Fox River bridge at St. Charles on the Fourth of July 1962. It would seem the fishing is good this holiday weekend, but the kids in the bottom photo were taking a dangerous chance. *(R.E. Puta, M. Finzer collection)*

*(Above and below)* Manifest No. 143 was east of St. Charles and had crossed the Fox River bridge on March 13, 1966, with spotless F3A 108C and five other F units on a fine late winter day. *(C.H. Zeiler)*

In the era of friction bearing wheels on freight cars derailments caused by burned off journals occurred all too frequently as near St. Charles in June 1960. On long trains, equipment and lading damage was severe, but there were seldom any employees injured. This wreck is serious enough to summon the CGW's 250-ton wrecker, X-250, from Chicago to assist in opening the line, with freight trains detouring in the meantime. Today, one of the contract wreck clearing outfits would be called to open the line. (K. Gause)

 **VIRGIL**

*(Left)* Eastbound manifest No. 192 was headed up by F3A 101C, one of the first 18 F3s delivered in October 1947, and five others as it passed through Virgil, 41.3 miles from the Chicago Transfer yard in October 1958.

*(Jim Konas, J.J. Buckley collection)*

 **RICHARDSON**

*(Below)* Often-photographed "doodlebug" 1009 was taken at Richardson, IL a point just west of Virgil on Train No. 3 on June 11, 1950. Shortly after this photo was exposed Richardson was discontinued as a station. *(G.E. Lloyd)*

# SYCAMORE

*(Right and below)* Two views of Baldwin DS4-4-1000 switch engine 34 taken at Sycamore on November 21, 1959. This 1000 h.p. unit was one of ten acquired in 1949 that dieselized practically all yard operations. *(G.E. Lloyd)*

*(Below)* CGW still employed five people at the Sycamore depot on June 23, 1962, to take care of local freight customers and handle train orders. The station was 56.6 miles from Chicago. *(R.E. Puta, M. Finzer collection)*

## CLARE

*(Right)* Moving along the Chicago District, Clare was 64.1 miles from the Chicago Central station. In 1958, the office was open from 845 p.m. to 545 a.m. in contrast to the daylight hours observed at most stations. Having an occasional night train order office assisted train dispatchers in the movement of trains. After Clare was closed, the station building was leased to a fertilizer dealer.

*(R.E. Puta, M. Finzer collection)*

## ESMOND

*(Below)* The snow is coming down furiously as a freight train passed the depot at Esmond, 5.7 miles west of Clare in December 1964. In 1958, office hours at Esmond were from 8 a.m. to 5 p.m. *(R.E. Puta, M. Finzer collection)*

## STILLMAN VALLEY

*(Left)* Stillman Valley was a non-agency station 83.4 miles from Chicago. The small station building was maintained for the convenience of track workers or signal maintainers.
*(R.E. Puta, M. Finzer collection)*

*(Below)* F3A 107C led five F units, 141 cars, totaling 8245 tons on Manifest No. 192 near Stillman Valley, IL on October 16, 1965. TOFC or piggyback traffic provided considerable revenues for CGW including "reefer" vans loaded with meat which outnumber packer "reefer" cars, on No. 192.
*(Mike Nelson)*

 HOLCOMB

*(Above)* Manifest freight 192 is climbing Holcomb hill west of Holcomb, IL, on June 6, 1966. "Six regulars" led by F3A 107A roll 121 cars towards Chicago. CGW operators and enginemen used the term "regulars" in reference to their covered wagons. *(Mike Nelson)*

 **BYRON**

*(Above)* Within two months, Chicago Great Western would be history, when F3A 111A, which had twenty years seniority, made a set out of a single boxcar at Byron in May 1968. Talk about being overpowered! *(Randy Garnhart)*

*(Below)* Some late winter snow remains on the ground on a gloomy day in March 1967 as No. 192 passes Byron. F3A 112C is controlling the five-unit engine consist.
*(Randy Garnhart)*

*(Above)* A westbound freight passes the old wooden depot at German Valley, IL in May 1968, as agent Grover Cain returns the wave of a trainman on the bay window caboose. German Valley was 100.9 miles west of Chicago's Grand Central Station. *(Randy Garnhart)*

 **SOUTH FREEPORT**

*(Above)* Three shiny new SD40s, with 405 in control, plus at least one F unit were in charge of westbound manifest 143 at South Freeport in October 1966. The nine SD40s received in 1966, were the heaviest and most powerful of CGW diesel power, and CGW's only other representative of the "second generation" of diesel locomotives. *(Randy Garnhart)*

*(Below)* The depot building at South Freeport had been replaced with a wooden sign when 113C, a late model F3A built in February 1949 powered No. 143 westbound, on a spring day in May 1968. *(Randy Garnhart)*

# PEARL CITY

*(Right)* The concrete block depot Pearl City, IL, 120 miles west of Chicago was closed before this photo was taken in August 1965. A train wreck in 1948 destroyed the old wooden depot.
*(R.E. Puta, M. Finzer collection)*

# STOCKTON

*(Below)* Stockton, IL, 123.4 miles west of Chicago Transfer, and 114.7 miles east of Oelwein was the freight train crew terminal on the Chicago District. Passenger train crews ran through between Chicago-Oelwein, however engine crews changed. During steam days East Stockton had a 21 track yard and a 15 stall engine house with a 200 ton coal chute, ice house and car repair shop. All were removed in 1948. On March 9, 1966, agent Chuck Finch watches engineer Glen Heitter ease 175 cars of #91 out of Stockton. *(Mike Nelson)*

*(Above)* GP30 202 and three mates bring No. 192 into Stockton from Oelwein in July 1967. Note the white company station wagon with the "Lucky Strike" logo on the door. *(Randy Garnhart)*

*(Below)* A few days after the July 1, 1968 merger with the Chicago & North Western there are no visible changes at Stockton as No. 91 with veteran F3A 111A does some switching by the classic tower. This building was once the yard office at East Stockton. It was moved to Stockton in 1936 to serve as the Eastern Division Dispatcher's Office. *(Randy Garnhart)*

 *(Above and below)* Two more views of CGW operations at Stockton a few days after the July 1, 1968 merger with C&NW, and a time that loyal Great Western employees were concerned about their futures. Two four-unit sets of high mileage Fs await some of their final calls to pull freight trains. *(Randy Garnhart)*

 **WINSTON TUNNEL**

*(Above)* The engineer has opened the cab window for a breath of fresh air after exiting the east portal of the half mile long Winston tunnel on No. 192 on March 13, 1966. Six F units with 101C ahead are powering 122 cars, weighing 7855 tons. *(Mike Nelson)*

*(Left and above)* Smoke similar to that left in the bore by the big Texas-type steam power for two decades, is coming from the east portal of Winston tunnel, as No. 192 exits on October 8, 1966. An 8560 ton train of 120 loads and 18 empties, including 23 TOFC, trails the straining units on the near one percent grade.

*(Mike Nelson)*

*(Above)* Spring was only two days old, on March 23, 1967 when No. 192, with six units, controlled by F3A 114A left the east portal of Winston tunnel pulling 125 Chicago-bound cars. *(Mike Nelson)*

*(Below)* A track motor car with a section gang enters the west portal for ice removal on February 5, 1966. *(Mike Nelson)*

In late 1965 early 1966 the CGW fan could still find plenty of F-unit action around the remote Winston tunnel.
*(Above)* On New Years Eve 1965 the 107A popped out of the portal and past the brick ventilating structure with #91. The west portal was by far the more difficult to photograph as the sun only was "right" during a narrow window of the day. And, of course, nothing ran then.
*(Below)* No. 192 approaches from the other way with the 112C leading on a more bleak February 5, 1966. *(Both, Mike Nelson)*

*(Above and below)* Along the Mississippi River backwaters on December 4, 1965 at Portage, westbound No. 91 had F3A 110C, four booster units and 103A moving a lengthy CGW train of 186 cars, 8315 tons. In the three years they were photographing the CGW in this area, the photographer and his brother only saw two trains of 186 cars. The Chicago line was not the route for those huge 180 car freights. They occurred most frequently on the line north of Oelwein.

*(Both, Mike Nelson)*

*(Above)* In this idyllic view, this time on a summer day, June 15, 1966, No. 91 heads west with 116 cars. *(Mike Nelson)*

*(Below)* Manifest train 192, with four GP30s led by 204 was passing Portage tower on July 10, 1966 with 142 cars, 8480 tons. CGW used Burlington trackage between Galena Jct. and Portage, 1/2 mile, thence the Illinois Central between Portage and Dubuque Jct. on the west side of the Mississippi River, another 13.8 miles. *(Mike Nelson)*

*(Above)* February 12, 1967, found Manifest No. 91 near East Dubuque, on Illinois Central trackage, with F3A 114C heading up the normal six units. *(T.E. Hoffman)*

*(Below)* F3A 114C, built in February 1949, was still working near the end of the independent CGW on April 11, 1968, as it led 124 cars out of the east portal of the Illinois Central tunnel at East Dubuque, IL. *(Mike Nelson)*

 **DUBUQUE**

*(Above)* No. 91 crossed the Mississippi River at Dubuque on IC trackage rights on December 3, 1967. 101 cars trail the six F unit engine consist, with F3A 115C in control. *(Mike Nelson)*

*(Below)* The Mississippi River was out of its banks at Dubuque, IA on April 25, 1952, as the Friday morning meat extra east passed with F3A 106C heading the four-unit engine consist. Thursdays were the heavy meat loading days in Iowa, and CGW ran a meat extra in advance of No. 192 on Friday into Chicago to make the night connections of the Eastern railroads, affording Sunday arrival on the East Coast, with the cars unloaded for Monday morning delivery. Before the Interstate Highway System was built, the railroads literally fed America. *(W.L. Heitter)*

*(Above)* Manifest train 55, with five units, and a block of the older flat cars, with two short trailers, passed by the Shot Tower at Dubuque on April 1, 1952. F3A 115A in the original diesel paint scheme is on the "point." The Shot Tower was built in 1856 to manufacture lead buck shot, and was saved for historical purposes by a public fund drive in 1959. *(W.L. Heitter)*

*(Below)* Manifest No. 192 was west of Dubuque on May 4, 1967, with F3A 106A heading a short 86-car train into Quigley's Cut. *(Mike Nelson)*

 **FAIRGROUND**

*(Above)* Passenger train No. 8, the only Oelwein-Chicago service on April 29, 1952 passed Fairground, IA on the west side of Dubuque, with FP7 116A, built by EMD in December 1950 powering a five-car train. FP7s 116A and 116C were the only FP7s on the CGW diesel roster.

(W.L. Heitter)

 **DURANGO**

*(Left)* Manifest No. 192 passed through Split Rock, near Durango, IA, which was 180.1 miles from Chicago Grand Central Station on May 31, 1968. Three SD40s, with 403 ahead, are moving the 70-car train east through the scenic hills of northeastern Iowa. *(Mike Nelson)*

*(Below)* Five Fs, with 116C ahead, roll No. 91 west of Durango on well-maintained track on August 25, 1966. The train is rather short—only 70 cars. *(Mike Nelson)*

*(Above)* No. 192 follows the Little Maquoketa River west of Durango on August 28, 1966. Six carloads of sheep bound for Sycamore, IL, trail the GP30s. *(Mike Nelson)*

*(Below)* No. 91 was east of Oelwein on September 13, 1952, to wind up our look at the Chicago District, Eastern Division, Chicago Great Western Railway Company. Note the vintage piggyback up front. *(W.L. Heitter)*

# Oelwein

On a vast railroad system such as a Santa Fe, Pennsylvania or Southern Pacific, also with the mega-merger giants of today, it would be difficult to pick a point on the railroad that was its "heart." On Chicago Great Western, even a novice at railroading would look at a map and select Oelwein, Iowa.

Oelwein got its start as the center of CGW operations when locomotive shops were moved from St. Paul and opened in April 1899. Future automobile magnate, Walter P. Chrysler, served as Superintendent of Motive Power with Oelwein headquarters from 1905 to 1910. Much important locomotive work was accomplished at Oelwein, with the building of three 2-6-6-2 Mallets from 2-6-2 Prairies in 1910, and the subsequent conversion of twenty 2-6-2s to 4-6-2s between 1910-1915. At all times, improvements were made to existing power as it went through the Oelwein shop for classified repairs. The shops were rebuilt and improved between 1933-1935 to handle the Texas type 2-10-4 locomotives, purchased in 1930-1931. Seven 2-8-0s and 2-8-2s were extensively rebuilt in 1941-1942, and all 36 2-10-4s were improved for 60 m.p.h. speeds with the application of light weight rods and disc main drivers.

At the car shop, "America's Premier Deluxe Motor Train," the BLUE BIRD was built in 1929 from old McKeen motor cars. The freight car shop handled general repairs to all freight cars, and work equipment.

Upon complete dieselization, heavy repair work to diesels was done at Oelwein, and a new running repair and service facility was constructed.

During the Deramus era, most offices were consolidated at the "Hub City" commencing with the train dispatchers in 1949, who occupied a new building adjacent to the passenger station. In 1951, operating, accounting, purchasing, freight claims and engineering departments were moved from Chicago. By 1953, all departments were in Oelwein except industrial, personnel and treasury headquartered in Kansas City. The President's office, and the legal department moved from Chicago to Kansas City in 1956. The Traffic Department stayed in Chicago.

The car shop suffered major damage in a fire on January 28, 1960 however a new facility was built, maintaining Oelwein's status as the "Hub City" of the CGW until the July 1, 1968 merger with the Chicago & North Western.

*(Above)* Veteran McKeen motor car 1003, built in 1910, was working Trains 35-36 between Oelwein and Clarion on May 28, 1949 with the landmark smoke stack of the Oelwein shops in the background. Sykes trailer MT-210 usually accompanied the 1003 on its 199 mile round trip.

*(J.J. Buckley)*

*(Left)* The following year, on July 26, 1950, the 1003 and trailer MT-210 was making its final trip to Clarion when it prepared to leave Oelwein with Conductor Johnny Fleming dressed in overalls instead of the usual passenger trainman's uniform.

*(W.L. Heitter)*

*(Above)* No. 91, the Oelwein-Council Bluffs through freight cleared the Oelwein yard on the afternoon of November 30, 1952 with F3 111C and an unidentified "B" unit pulling four flat cars of T.O.F.C. and unreported miscellaneous freight. *(W.L. Heitter)*

*(Below)* On March 22, 1958, at Oelwein, about 20 flat cars of TOFC, or "piggyback" traffic await movement. The Pabst trailer was in service of the St. Paul brewer handling beer. An early advocate of "piggyback" (in 1936), CGW by the mid-1950s was fourth in number of trailers handled, ranking only behind the larger Southern Pacific, Pennsylvania and New York, New Haven & Hartford. *(W.L. Heitter)*

*(Above)* On October 18, 1959, the morning sun shines on the maroon nose, with the familiar CGW emblem of FP7 116A. Built in December 1950, it was renumbered to C&NW 218, and in the mid-1980s was repainted to the original CGW livery and placed on display at Oelwein as a monument to former CGW railroaders. *(L. Keyser)*

*(Below)* One of the Great Western's early diesels 600 h.p.SC No. 7 built by Electro Motive in August 1936 was assigned to the "Ping Pong Run" local which ran out of Oelwein on June 7, 1952 to Sumner, on the St. Paul line, then worked to Wavery on the Omaha line, before returning to Oelwein. *(W.L. Heitter)*

*(Above)* FP7 116A and a sister prepare to leave Oelwein for Dubuque on October 18, 1959, on a rare Great Western passenger excursion sponsored by the Iowa Chapter, National Railway Historical Society. CGW borrowed three Great Northern coaches to accommodate the 262 riders. *(L. Keyser)*

*(Below)* One of ten Baldwin DS4-4-1000 switchers, built in 1949, engine 34 was stored at Oelwein on August 6, 1961. 34 was not renumbered by C&NW, but Nos. 32, 38 and 39 became C&NW 1073, 1074 and 1075. *(G.E. Lloyd)*

*(Above)* Two paint variations of switchers at Oelwein on August 7, 1962. No. 27 was a 1000 h.p. EMD NW2 built in June 1948, and not renumbered by the C&NW in 1968. No. 53 was a 1500 h.p. Alco RS2, built in September 1949, and also did not receive a new number. *(Roger E. Puta, M. Finzer collection)*

*(Below)* The modern CGW passenger station at Oelwein as it appeared on August 7, 1962. With the Deramus era, CGW had more new modern stations than most of its competition. *(Roger E. Puta, M. Finzer collection)*

*(Above)* NW2s 28 and 30 were MU'ed at Oelwein on August 7, 1962 to handle the heavy switching on the yard lead, instead of the usual "cow-calf" combination. No. 30 would become C&NW 1016, however No. 28 remained with its CGW number. *(Roger E. Puta, M. Finzer collection)*

*(Below)* In this view of the Oelwein locomotive shop on August 7, 1962, a retired gas-electric motor car had been de-trucked and used as a storage shed. The orange maintenance-of-way equipment includes the diner used with the Oelwein wrecker outfit. *(Roger E. Puta, M. Finzer collection)*

*(Above)* An overhead view from the yardmaster's tower of the Oelwein yard and supporting facilities, looking northwest on August 7, 1962. From the left bottom are the dispatcher's office, Railway express building and passenger station. Combine 262 stands on the business car track. NW2s 28 and 30 await the next switching assignment chore. The ice house and dock are in the center. The old roundhouse and the new in 1961 car shop appear in the distance. A neat and modern CGW facility at the "Hub City." *(Roger E. Puta, M. Finzer collection)*

*(Right)* Looking southeast from the yardmaster's tower at Oelwein on August 7, 1962. The Chicago district is tangent to the left and the Kansas City district goes to the right. Stored passenger equipment and two business or office cars are in the center. The general office building appears at the top of the locomotive shop. *(Roger E. Puta, M. Finzer collection)*

*(Above)* Another August 7, 1962 overhead view of the locomotive shop at Oelwein with various equipment including the 250-ton wrecking derrick and F-units awaiting assignment.
*(Roger E. Puta, M. Finzer collection)*

*(Below)* Oelwein was still a good place to watch "F" units on August 7, 1962. Some were stored, but CGW still rostered a total of 74 "F" units, but only two Geeps. New second generation GP30s would come next year. *(Roger E. Puta, M. Finzer collection)*

Continuing our tour of Oelwein on August 7, 1962, F3A 110 is outside the diesel running repair shop with stored passenger equipment next to the yardmaster's tower. *(Roger E. Puta, M. Finzer collection)*

*(Above)* Gas-electric motor car 1000 served as the Winona, MN yard switcher, however on August 7, 1962 it was at Oelwein for some shop attention.
*(Roger E. Puta, M. Finzer collection)*

*(Left)* A side view of the nose of F3A 110 through the vestibule door of stored combination car 286 on August 7, 1962. The 110 left EMD in March 1948 to help put the big 2-10-4s on the storage tracks, also at Oelwein.
*(Roger E. Puta, M. Finzer collection)*

*(Above)* Maroon caboose 604 was a 27 foot long car, one of 24, built by Pullman-Standard in 1946 and dubbed an "Eastern style cab." On August 7, 1962 it was on the Oelwein "rip" track. *(W.J. Dunlap)*

*(Below)* CGW rostered ten 2000 h.p. E.M.D. TR-2 (transfer) switchers, bought in 1948-49 for heavy switching service. So called "cow-calf" 60A-60B was on hand at Oelwein on October 15, 1962.
*(Bill Volkmer collection)*

*(Above)* Great Western ventured into yard dieselization early when it acquired Baldwin-Westinghouse 800 h.p. No. 2 in December 1934. It was rebuilt by Electro Motive Corporation in December 1941 and de-rated to 720 h.p. On May 13, 1966, the veteran switcher was laid-up at Oelwein and it would be sold for scrap in October 1966.
*(J.J. Buckley)*

*(Above)* As would be expected, Oelwein was the home of the 250-ton wrecking derrick, appropriately numbered X-250. Fs of various hues, plus a solitary GP7 are on hand, waiting for tonnage to be switched for outbound trains on a spring day in 1964. *(Roger E. Puta, M. Finzer collection)*

*(Above)* "Cow-calf" TR2 64A-64B was busy switching at Oelwein on September 16, 1966. None of the nine TR2 sets were incorporated into the C&NW roster, retaining CGW numbers until retirement. *(J.J. Buckley)*

*(Below)* On a dull March 11, 1967, four-year-old GP30 207 was outside the diesel house at Oelwein. Upon the July 1, 1968 merger it became C&NW 807.
*(Roger E. Puta, M. Finzer collection)*

*(Above)* With the only diesel repair facility on the CGW at Oelwein, it follows that all locomotives could be found there. TR2 62A-62B were in need of paint when photographed on May 20, 1967. *(K.C. Henkels, R.J. Yanosey collection)*

*(Below)* A general view of the diesel running repair shop at Oelwein in August 1967. A five-unit set of veteran "Fs" headed by 111A built by E.M.D. in May 1948 will soon be on the road handling a freight train to Chicago, St. Paul, Kansas City or Council Bluffs from the "Hub City" of the CGW

*(L. Keyser)*

# COUNCIL BLUFFS-OMAHA

As the last of the six trans-Iowa railroads that reached Council Bluffs (in November 1903), Chicago Great Western benefited little from the tremendous tonnage brought to the Missouri River by the Union Pacific. With its longer route and non-competitive perishable schedule, CGW mostly handled tonnage destined to CGW destinations and did little "bridge" business.

A yard and an 11-stall roundhouse were built in Council Bluffs, with a freight house and another yard, mostly serving grain elevators, in Omaha. These facilities were reached by trackage rights over the UP and CGW passenger trains used the Burlington station in Omaha.

Omaha meat packers, for many years, divided their Chicago gateway traffic with the six railroads, giving each most of the tonnage on one day of the week. CGW "meat night" was Thursday and on that day, during the diesel era, two additional units were placed on No. 91 at Oelwein to protect the Thursday night meat extra.

A terminal program in the mid-1950s saw a new yard with longer tracks constructed in southeast Council Bluffs. A new brick passenger station was opened in January 1956, and a new two-stall engine house and a wye for turning motive power were added in 1957. These new facilities were adequate until the 1968 merger with Chicago & North Western, at which time they were abandoned. The depot became a local bar named "The Depot" and the roundhouse was acquired by a bulk oil company.

Passenger service to Council Bluffs-Omaha ended when Trains 13-14, to and from the Twin Cities were discontinued on September 30, 1965.

## COUNCIL BLUFFS

*(Above)* NW2 #27 at Council Bluffs, delivered in June 1948, was one of seventeen diesel switchers of that model delivered by E.M.D. in 1948-1949. *(Lou Schmitz)*

*(Above)* F3A 152 was tied up by the steam era mechanical facilities in Council Bluffs on April 17, 1954. One of three F3As equipped for passenger train service, it would leave Omaha for Minneapolis on coach-only Train 14 at 730 p.m.
*(Carl Hehl, Lou Schmitz collection)*

*(Below)* The eleven-stall Council Bluffs roundhouse had not serviced a steam locomotive for over four years, when RS-2 #55 posed on July 31, 1954. CGW owned eight RS2s all purchased in 1949. Unfortunately for the railfans the CGW would never purchase from Alco again. *(Lou Schmitz)*

*(Above)* A four-unit set of fancy painted F3s was also on hand at Council Bluffs on July 31, 1954. Tonnage on Manifest trains 91-90 between Oelwein and Council Bluffs seldom required a 6000 h.p. locomotive. *(Lou Schmitz)*

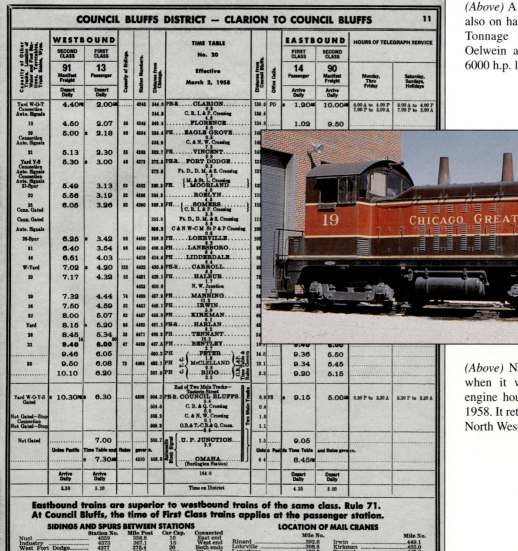

*(Above)* NW2 19 was a little over ten years old when it was spotted outside the one-year-old engine house at Council Bluffs on September 7, 1958. It retained its number 19 after the Chicago & North Western merger of 1968. *(Lou Schmitz)*

*(Above)* In the later simplified paint scheme, four Fs, controlled by engine 103 are east of Council Bluffs on manifest train 90 to Oelwein on May 19, 1962. *(Lou Schmitz)*

*(Below)* One unit was normally assigned to Trains 13-14, however on August 8, 1962 No. 13 was pulling into the Burlington station at Omaha powered by F7A 155 and F3A 152. In the earlier photograph at Council Bluffs in 1954, No. 152 was certainly better attired. *(Roger E. Puta, M. Finzer collection)*

*(Above)* Another angle of No. 13 at the Burlington station in Omaha on August 8, 1962. Mail and express traffic made most of the expenses to run this train and when the Post Office department cancelled the contract, Nos. 13-14 made their last trips on September 29, 1965.

(Roger E. Puta, M. Finzer collection)

*(Below)* One of the two former Milwaukee Road HIAWATHA coaches, purchased in 1961, was carrying the markers for Train 13 as it paused at Council Bluffs on August 8, 1962. The veteran flagman is prepared to furnish protection whenever required by Rule 99. *(Roger E. Puta, M. Finzer collection)*

*(Above)* F7A 153, which had left LaGrange in June 1949, had been recently repainted to the maroon simplified paint scheme when it laid over at Council Bluffs between runs on December 8, 1962.

*(Bill Volkmer collection)*

*(Right)* The later and last "covered wagon" paint scheme of solid red looked good when F3A 111A, F3B 102B and FP7 116A were called at Council Bluffs on the fine autumn day of October 18, 1963, to take Manifest train 90 east to Oelwein. *(L.E. Stagner)*

*(Above)* 111A-102B-116A were passing the east (or south) end of the Council Bluffs yard at 1:35 p.m. October 18, 1963 with the 64 cars of Train 90 in tow, starting the 259 mile march to Oelwein. *(L.E. Stagner)*

*(Below)* The maroon paint looked almost black on the middle unit of the three Fs tied up at Council Bluffs on February 8, 1964, waiting for a call to take manifest train 90 to Oelwein.
*(G.E. Lloyd)*

*(Above)* F7A 153 was on one end of the usual three-unit set that tied up at Council Bluffs between the arrival of No. 91 due at 1030 p.m. and the departure of No. 90 at 500 a.m. Fortunately for photographers, No. 90 was seldom called before 12 O'Clock noon. With few scheduled main line local freight trains, and the emphasis on gross-ton-miles-per-train-hour of the Deramus/Reidy management eras, maintenance of schedules did not receive high priority, except in the case of making connections at Chicago with meat traffic. *(Bill Volkmer collection)*

*(Below)* No. 14 was made up at the Burlington station in Omaha behind F7A 156 alongside an eastbound Burlington train on August 18, 1964. *(G.E. Lloyd)*

*(Above)* CGW passenger service to Omaha/Council Bluffs had just over 30 days before its end, when No. 13 pulled away from the Council Bluffs station for Omaha on the morning of August 28, 1965, behind F3A 150. There would still be freight tonnage for 150 to move. *(Lou Schmitz)*

*(Below)* The last rays of sunshine on December 11, 1966 are about to leave, when No. 90 left Council Bluffs with the usual three Fs in charge. *(Lou Schmitz)*

# MASON CITY DISTRICT

## Chicago Great Western Railway

### March 2, 1958

| | Depart Daily | Capacity | Station | Distance Hay | | | Distance Cou | Office | Arrive Daily | Thru Friday | Sundays, Holidays |
|---|---|---|---|---|---|---|---|---|---|---|---|
| Yard W-O-T-Y | 10.40 PM | | 3081 | 0 | PH-R | HAYFIELD | 260.6 | HB | s 4.55 AM | 5.00 AM to 1.00 PM / 9.00 PM to 5.00 AM | (Saturdays only) 5.00 AM to 1.00 PM / 9.00 PM to 5.00 AM |
| 13 Auto. Signals | | | | 12.7 | | 12.7 C. M. St. P. & P. Crossing | 247.9 | | | | |
| Connection Auto. Signals | | | | 15.9 | PH | 3.2 C. M. St. P. & P. Crossing | 244.7 | | | | |
| Yard-S | s 11.15 | 68 | 3098 | 17.5 | PH-R | 1.6 AUSTIN | 243.1 | AU | s 4.25 | 8.45 PM to 5.45 AM | 8.45 PM to 5.45 AM |
| Connection Not Gated-10 | f 11.35 | 56 | 3109 | 28.3 | PH | 10.8 { I. C. R. R. Crossing } LYLE | 232.3 | PX | f 4.00 | 8.00 AM to 5.00 PM | |
| 30 | 12.20 | | 3129 | 48.2 | PH | 19.9 MANLY | 212.4 | JU | 3.15 | Continuous | Continuous |
| Connection Interlocked | | | | 48.4 | | 0.2 C. R. I. & P.-M. St. L. Crossings | 212.2 | | | | |
| | | 66 | | 48.9 | | 0.5 West Manly | 211.7 | | | | |
| Connection Auto. Signals | SEE JOINT TIME TABLE | 55 | | 56.4 | PH | 7.5 North Yard | 204.2 | SEE JOINT TIME TABLE | | | |
| | | | | 57.0 | | 0.6 C. & N. W. Crossing | 203.6 | | | | |
| Yard W-O-S | | W-19 E-47 | 3139 | 57.6 | PH | 0.6 MASON CITY | 203.0 | DF | | 8.00 AM to 5.00 PM | |
| Connection Auto. Signals | | | | 58.5 | | 0.9 C. M. St. P. & P. Crossing | 202.1 | | | | |
| Connection Interlocked | 12.48 | 18 | 3141 | 59.1 | PH-R | 0.6 { CLEAR LAKE JCT. } M. C. & C. L. Crossing | 201.5 | K | 2.35 | Continuous | Continuous |
| 23 | 1.09 | | 3153 | 71.2 | PH | 12.1 SWALEDALE | 189.4 | SW | 2.13 | 8.00 AM to 5.00 PM | |
| 15 | 1.17 | 56 | 3157 | 75.8 | PH | 4.6 THORNTON | 184.8 | PZ | 2.05 | 8.00 AM to 5.00 PM | |
| 18 | 1.26 | | 3163 | 81.3 | PH | 5.5 MESERVEY | 179.3 | VZ | 1.55 | 8.00 AM to 5.00 PM | |
| Connection Not Gated | | | | 89.3 | | 8.0 C. R. I. & P. Crossing | 171.3 | | | | |

## AUSTIN

*(Above)* Alco RS2 No. 56 had the Hayfield-Austin "turn" moving at milepost 1 of the Mason City District, on the late afternoon of July 16, 1963, with six empty Hormel refrigerator cars for the plant at Austin included in the nine car consist. *(W.J. Dunlap)*

*(Below)* Another view of RS2 56, while switching at Austin on the Hayfield-Austin turnaround in September 1963. Besides the Hormel meat packing plant, CGW served other industries. *(W.J. Dunlap)*

*(Above)* RS2 51, built by Alco in September 1949, was at Austin on August 26, 1952 while working from Hayfield. No. 51 was still on the CGW roster along with the eight other engines of that type when CGW merged with C&NW July 1, 1968.
*(W.L. Heitter)*

*(Below)* Austin, MN was another CGW point that featured a new attractive depot built during the Deramus administration. On August 26, 1962, Nos. 13-14 still made stops while enroute between Omaha and Minneapolis.
*(R.E. Puta, M. Finzer collection)*

## MASON CITY

*(Above)* Mason City, 57.6 miles from Hayfield, and 42.4 miles from Clarion, also had enough local switching to keep a yard engine crew assigned. In August 1966, NW-2 No. 31, a March 1949 delivery from EMD. was tied up between assignments.
*(Randy Garnhart)*

*(Right)* The attractive brick depot at Mason City, IA was used jointly with the Chicago, Rock Island & Pacific, which on August 13, 1967 operated four daily trains, compared with the CGW offering of freight service only. *(R.E. Puta, M. Finzer collection)*

## CLEAR LAKE JUNCTION

*(Right)* The Clear Lake Junction station was closed permanently at the time this photo was exposed on August 12, 1967. Clear Lake Junction was located 41 miles from the end of the Mason City district at Clarion.
*(R.E. Puta, M. Finzer collection)*

# MANKATO DISTRICT

*(Right)* The CGW Mankato District extended 67.4 miles between Randolph and Mankato, MN, with the Minneapolis, Northfield & Southern having trackage rights between Randolph and Northfield Jct. 8.5 miles. Way freight trains 121-122 operated six days a week and usually met at Faribault. On June 12, 1967, one of these trains was powered by RS2 No. 51, which was switching at Northfield, 8.7 miles out of Randolph and a crossing with the Milwaukee Road.
*(Bill Volkmer collection)*

*(Below)* S1 No. 11 was the other locomotive in way freight service through Northfield MN on June 12, 1967. The little 660 h.p. "goat" was equipped with classification signal lights for branch line operation. It was built by Alco-GE in June 1948 and became C&NW 1216 upon the CGW-C&NW merger.
*(Bill Volkmer collection)*

# Winona Branch

*(Above)* The Winona branch diverged from the McIntire District at Simpson, MN and extended 50.2 miles to Winona. With 10 to 15 m.p.h. maximum speeds on the March 2, 1958 Minnesota division timetable, it was obviously of light construction and poorly maintained. A rare yard engine was used at Winona. 300 h.p. gas-electric motor car 1000, originally a McKeen Co. car built in 1910, was the regular assigned engine. On June 24, 1962 it was tied-up between switch "tricks."
*(R.D. Sims)*

*(Left)* Another view, made on December 4, 1962 found Motor 1000 pulling one of Swift & Company's attractive refrigerator cars out of the plant on a gloomy day along the Mississippi River.
*(W.J. Dunlap)*

*(Above and below)* Two views of the Winona branch way freight with RS2 No. 55 on February 1, 1964 indicate a fairly reasonable freight business was still handled at Winona, a point also served by the Burlington, The Milwaukee Road, Chicago & North Western and the Green Bay & Western. *(Both-W.J. Dunlap)*

### Iowa and Minnesota Branch Lines

| Randolph—Mankato<br>Freight Service Only | | Waverly—Sumner<br>Freight Service Only | | Winona—Rochester<br>Freight Service Only | |
|---|---|---|---|---|---|
| Mls | **TABLE 7** | Mls | **TABLE 8** | Mls | **TABLE 10** |
| | Central Time | | Central Time | | Central Time |
| 0 | **Randolph** | 0 | **Waverly** | 0 | **Winona** |
| 7 | Waterford | 6 | Bremer | 23 | Altura |
| 9 | **Northfield** | 13 | Tripoli | 27 | Bethany |
| 12 | Dundas | 18 | Spring Fountain | 32 | Utica |
| 16 | Bridgewater | 22 | **Sumner 1** | 37 | St. Charles |
| 23 | **Faribault** | | | 41 | Dover |
| 32 | Warsaw | | | 51 | Predmore |
| 35 | Morristown | | | 56 | Simpson 3 |
| 41 | **Waterville** | | | 63 | **Rochester 3** |
| 47 | Elysian | | | | |
| 54 | Madison Lake | **McIntire—Osage**<br>Freight Service Only | | **Fort Dodge—Gypsum**<br>Freight Service Only | |
| 61 | Watters | | | | |
| 66 | Benning | Mls | **TABLE 9** | Mls | **TABLE 11** |
| 70 | **Mankato** | 0 | McIntire, Ia. | 0 | Fort Dodge |
| | | 8 | Little Cedar | 4.5 | Gypsum |
| | | 16 | Osage | | |

# McIntire District

With the 141.2 miles extending from Randolph to McIntire, thence to Osage, this district allowed the Chicago Great Western to serve the large Minnesota city of Rochester, when it acquired the Winona and Southwestern in 1901. As the home for the Mayo Clinic, Rochester became an important passenger station and for many years through sleepers were operated between Rochester and both Chicago and Kansas City. The Kansas City sleeper lasted until 1949. Iron ore mines were located at Stewartville and CGW moved iron ore south to mills in the Chicago and St. Louis areas. Other freight handled included grain, canned foods and grain mill products. The Pine Island-Red Wing segment, of 31 miles was abandoned, with the last train operating May 5, 1965. Thereafter local turnarounds were operated from Randolph and McIntire to serve remaining customers. The 15.8 miles from the St. Paul District at McIntire to Osage was abandoned April 10, 1967 after years of light traffic and deferred maintenance. Since the line via Rochester was a "loop" it was also used occasionally for detour purposes when the St. Paul District was out-of-service, until May 1965. In 1958, freight train speed limits on most portions of the District were 30 to 35 m.p.h. The McIntire-Osage portion was down to 10 m.p.h.

*(Above)* On a cold day in the late winter of 1964, RS2 engine 52 had a healthy consist of 18 cars on the way freight between Randolph and Cannon Falls. *(Jim Gensmer)*

 *(Above)* A gloomy November 20, 1965 found RS2 number 55 on the McIntire district way freight with a seven-car train at the depot at Cannon Falls, MN.
*(Thomas Hoffman)*

*(Left)* Also on November 20, 1965, photographer Hoffman found S1 switcher 15 tied up at Red Wing. The 660 h.p. Alco-G.E. unit was built in June 1948 and renumbered to C&NW 1220.
*(Thomas Hoffman)*

*(Above)* S1 engine 12 is dwarfed by the grain elevator of the Fleishmann company at Red Wing on July 21, 1963. There was still enough carload traffic at Red Wing to keep a regular switch engine crew assigned. *(Walter Dunlap)*

*(Below)* While based at Rochester, S1 13 was doing some switching at Goodhue, 16 miles south of Red Wing on the McIntire District, on January 30, 1964. The crew was enjoying some caboose cooked oyster stew before returning to Rochester. *(Roger E. Puta, M. Finzer collection)*

*(Above)* S1 13 was handling only "Eastern caboose" 609 when it passed through the small Minnesota town of Zumbrota on January 30, 1964. *(Walter Dunlap)*

## ROCHESTER

The two-stall roundhouse at Rochester on December 6, 1963 hosted S1 13 and RS2 55, as a three-unit set of Fs, headed by 107A await to be called. *(Walter Dunlap)*

*(Above)* A mechanic was giving some attention to RS2 55 tied up at Rochester on December 6, 1963. The new paint on the front and the trucks had been applied as a result of a recent encounter with an automobile at a crossing. 55 was Alco's builder number 77187 of September 1949 and was among five units that almost finished off active CGW steam power. *(Walter Dunlap)*

*(Below)* F-units were also used on the McIntire District. The 115C, an old F3 built in February 1949 as CGW wound up main line freight dieselization, was tied up at Rochester on August 7, 1962. The main building of the Mayo Clinic can be seen in the background. *(Roger E. Puta, M. Finzer collection)*

*(Above)* F3A 107A and two other F7s were southbound with an extra handling two empty boxcars and a caboose as they passed the Libby plant at Rochester on December 6, 1963. *(Walter Dunlap)*

*(Below)* Two "Eastern" cabooses and S1 12 were tied up at Rochester on June 24, 1964 awaiting the next day's chores of switching and handling way freight trains. The summer weeds are rapidly taking over the CGW right-of-way. *(Walter Dunlap)*

Slow moving RS2 51 is aggravating the motorists in downtown Rochester on May 23, 1963, as the 1500 h.p. Alco-GE handles a way freight to Randolph. *(Walter Dunlap)*

*(Below)* The McIntire-Rochester way freight No. 126 powered by three F units was switching at Simpson on a fall day in October 1960. Simpson was 40 miles out of McIntire and 7.6 miles from Rochester where the crew would tie-up. Three unit F combinations were normal on Trains 125-126. *(Walter Dunlap)*

*(Above)* The December 6, 1963, Rochester-McIntire extra with F3A 107A in the lead passed Simpson with its light consist, late on a winter afternoon. *(Walter Dunlap, R.D. Sims collection)*

*(Below)* South of Simpson, F3A 107A continues its slow trek to McIntire, on the nice winter afternoon of December 6, 1963. *(Walter Dunlap)*

 **STEWARTVILLE**

*(Above)* The well maintained frame depot at Stewartville, MN on August 7, 1962. The old baggage truck had not been needed for years, but it was still on the platform.
*(Roger E. Puta, M. Finzer collection)*

 **RACINE**

*(Right)* Racine, MN was 28.5 miles north of McIntire and its standard CGW frame depot was still manned by an agent who worked from 8 AM to 5 PM Monday thru Friday as on this August 7, 1962. Perhaps the main track with its weeds almost covering the rails, was one example of why Chicago Great Western was often called "The Great Weedy?"
*(Roger E. Puta, M. Finzer collection)*

# TWIN CITIES

A.B. Stickney's Minnesota and Northwestern was constructed south from St. Paul commencing in September 1884. The Minnesota and Northwestern became the Chicago St. Paul and Kansas City in December 1887, reaching three of the four principal terminals. The CStP&KC formed the nucleus of the Chicago Great Western, when the CGW was incorporated on July 1, 1892.

St. Paul-Minneapolis soon became the second most important CGW interchange, with a heavy movement to and from the Great Northern, Northern Pacific and Soo Line, which fed forest products and grain to the CGW. Flour milled in the Minneapolis mills and packing house products also moved south on the CGW to connections at Chicago, Kansas City and Council Bluffs. After World War II, paper products became an important commodity received off the connections. Rock Island was the most important competitor with CGW for tonnage moving south inasmuch as the CRI&P also served the same gateways as CGW. During the steam era, three manifest freight trains departed the State Street yard near South St. Paul daily. Dieselization reduced service to trains 41 and 43 to Oelwein where connections were made south, east and west. Nos. 42 and 92 were Oelwein to St. Paul trains handling petroleum products, grain, meat originating from St. Joseph and Waterloo, and general merchandise. A turnaround local operated out of State Street yard to Rosemount, 17.3 miles serving a large oil refinery at Roseport. Transfer runs operated to the Minnesota Transfer yard, which served as a clearing house for all connecting Twin Cities railroads. Passenger trains used the Great Northern station in Minneapolis, with trackage rights, also over the GN to and from the St. Paul Union Station. Engine facilities and light freight car repair tracks were also at State Street.

The importance of the Twin Cities to the CGW continued up to the 1968 merger with Chicago & North Western.

*(Below)* Passenger train No. 14 had a Union Pacific car of express from Omaha when it arrived at St. Paul on the morning of August 21, 1955 with passenger-equipped F7A 154 in charge of a five-car train.
*(Lou Schmitz)*

*(Right)* No. 6, from Kansas City, once the MILL CITIES LIMITED pulled into the St. Paul Union Depot on the morning of July 7, 1957, with the usual single 150-156 series F3A or F7A as power. *(Edward S. Miller)*

*(Below)* On a summer morning in July 1961, No. 14 from Omaha had about completed an overnight trip with F3A 152 and an unusual second unit when it arrived at the Great Northern station in Minneapolis. Burlington, C&NW, Minneapolis & St. Louis and Northern Pacific also used the GN facility.
*(Emery J. Gulash)*

 *(Above)* F3A 105A and five other Fs had the situation under control when they arrived at St. Paul on a snowy February 18, 1967 on No. 92. In fair weather, six Fs could bring 9950 tons from Hayfield into St. Paul. *(E. Kanak, Bill Volkmer collection)*

F3A 150, an F3A built by Electro-Motive Division in November 1948 was the first diesel unit acquired for passenger service. It was under the train shed at the Great Northern depot in Minneapolis in August 1965 between runs on Nos. 14-13. The last CGW passenger train would soon leave Minneapolis—on September 30, 1965. *(M.J. Herson)*

*(Above)* The morning of July 29, 1963, found F7A 153 bringing No. 14 into St. Paul. After a scheduled ten minute stop, No. 14 would use Great Northern trackage to reach its final terminal in Minneapolis. Nos. 13-14 were the last vestige of a once extensive CGW passenger train service and were still in the timetable only by the virtue of a U.S. Post Office Department mail contract. *(Don Ball collection)*

*(Below)* After cutting off from No. 92, the six Fs were awaiting service and a call back to Oelwein. A 9000 h.p. set of Fs were rated at 8200 tons to Hayfield, and 14,700 tons onto Oelwein. There was usually a big fill at Hayfield, and in the summer iron ore to pick up at McIntire. *(E. Kanak, Bill Volkmer collection)*

*(Above)* A side view of "calf" 59 at St. Paul's State Street engine terminal, also on June 2, 1968. 2000 h.p. TR2s 59AB had left EMD in July 1949, and still retained the original friction bearing trucks. *(Bill Volkmer collection)*

*(Below)* Chicago Great Western had less than a month of existence left on June 2, 1968 when a set of almost 20 year old F freight units waited at the State Street engine terminal, for a call to return to Oelwein. *(Bill Volkmer)*

*(Above)* Old F7s and young GP30s wait between runs at the State Street engine terminal, near South St. Paul during the last winter of CGW operation on January 13, 1968. Advances in diesel locomotive technology have resulted in a four unit set of GP30s developing the 9000 h.p. of six F units. However tonnage ratings favored six F7s with 24 instead of sixteen traction motors. *(E. Kanak collection)*

*(Below)* A variety of diesel power was on hand at the St. Paul State Street engine terminal on June 2, 1968. TR2 59A-B was in local service to Rosemount, and the Fs and GP30s waited for calls to return to Oelwein when tonnage was available. *(Joe Piersen)*

*(Above)* Two days before the end of the CGW, Baldwin DS4-4-1000 switcher #38 was on hand at the St. Paul engine terminal. The nineteen-year-old engine would be re-numbered to C&NW 1074 for a short sojourn of service, before its retirement. Seven of the ten Baldwin switchers would not be re-numbered. *(Bill Volkmer collection)*

*(Below)* Transfer work in the Twin Cities was heavy and always kept a couple of "cow-calf" TR2s such as the 66 busy. *(P.C. Winters)*

# St. Paul District

Chicago Great Western's St. Paul District included the 189 miles from Minneapolis, via St. Paul and Hayfield to Oelwein. Freight crews tied up at the State Street Yard, near South St. Paul. At Hayfield, the Mason City District to Clarion diverged. During the Deramus-Reidy eras of CGW management, passenger trains 5-6 operated between Oelwein-Minneapolis and Omaha trains 13-14 left or entered the St. Paul District at Hayfield. Manifest freight trains 41 and 43 operated south and Nos. 92 and 42 north between Oelwein and State Street. The only regular local service was provided between State Street and Rosemount. Southbound manifest trains handled primarily, lumber, grain, flour and packing house products with the northbound counterparts handling petroleum products, food products and general merchandise. Ore moving south from McIntire was picked up by No. 41 and in 1965 this train was handling 15,000 tons from McIntire to Oelwein. On the June 25, 1965, Minnesota Division dispatcher's sheet No. 41 handled 201 loads and 42 empties, 15,325 tons out of McIntire including 60 ore, 19 reefers, and 1 tri-level of Fords. CGW manifest trains handled the available traffic, regardless of its relative importance. This huge train was handled by the usual six F-units and it left State Street at 509PM and arrived Oelwein at 405AM on June 26th with pick-ups at Randolph, Hayfield, and McIntire. In the 1960's speed limits on the well-maintained St. Paul District were 60 m.p.h. for passenger trains and 45 or 50 for freights.

## Randolph

*(Below)* On a nice late summer day in September 1966, four GP30s, headed by 205 were rolling manifest train 43 southbound near Randolph. The eight GP30s, delivered during 1963, had resulted in seven F3s and one F7 being sent to Electro-Motive as trade-ins. *(Jim Konas, J.J. Buckley collection)*

 **KENYON**

*(Above)* Chasing No. 43, it was captured on film again as it rolled south through Kenyon MN, 51.7 miles from State Street later on that fall afternoon. Four GP30s equaled 9000 hp, the horsepower equivalent of six F-units.

*(Jim Konas, J.J. Buckley collection)*

*(Right)* GP30s were still a year away when No. 43 passed Kenyon on August 31, 1962. No. 43 was due out of State Street at 5 a.m. daily, with a 2:30 p.m. arrival at Oelwein where connections were made to Kansas City on Kansas City District No. 43 and to Chicago on No. 90. No. 43 picked up at Randolph and at Hayfield, including meat from packing plants at Austin.

*(Walter Dunlap)*

## DODGE CENTER

*(Above)* Late in the autumn day of September 29, 1962, No. 43 with F3A 103C, and four trailing units, handling 120 cars was near Dodge Center, MN, at Milepost, KC 449. No. 43 is not due to reach Kansas City until 215 PM September 30.

*(Walter Dunlap)*

 **HAYFIELD**

*(Right)* The large frame depot at Hayfield, MN, late on a September day in 1962. Hayfield, 80.8 miles from St. Paul Union Depot was the junction point with the Mason City District, and normally the four manifest trains made set-outs or pick-ups. *(Roger E. Puta, M. Finzer collection)*

*(Above)* In the diesel era, Hayfield had minimum mechanical facilities, including a two-stall engine house, turntable, sand and fuel oil. On a fall day in September 1962 it appeared to be dormant. *(Walter Dunlap)*

*(Below)* RS2 56 was in charge of the Hayfield-Austin turn on July 16, 1963. The Hormel packing plant at Austin divided its meat traffic between the CGW and The Milwaukee Road. Hormel meat routed via CGW, left Hayfield on No. 43. On August 15, 1963, 43 picked up seven meat for Chicago, and four for Kansas City. Although CGW freight schedules were slow, they were reliable with connections usually made, and hence the packers had no complaints. *(Walter Dunlap)*

It was bitter cold at Hayfield on March 9, 1963, as No. 43 pulled out for Oelwein with 151 cars in tow. The friction bearing journals would be slow to warm up and the crew hoped they wouldn't have to double any hills, on the run to Oelwein. *(Walter Dunlap)*

*(Top photo)* An unidentified RS2 was tied up at Hayfield at twilight on the short day of November 28, 1963. *(Walter Dunlap)*

*(Bottom photo)* A six-unit set of Fs, an RS2 and an isolated F were at the Hayfield engine terminal on the first day of June 1963. *(Walter Dunlap)*

 112 *(Above)* An attractive crimson F3A, 110C, delivered to the CGW in March 1948, to replace 2-10-4s, heads up a six-unit engine consist at Hayfield on January 31, 1964.
*(Walter Dunlap)*

*(Below)* A spring snow storm on April 11, 1965, found a late running No. 14 making its station stop at Hayfield, behind F3A 150. A six-car train and adverse weather called for two units instead of one. *(Walter Dunlap)*

 **NEW HAMPTON**

*(Above)* New Hampton, IA was 33.5 miles north of Oelwein, on the St. Paul District. The color light signal on the main track was green, also the newer type color light train order signal or "board" was clear. Automatic block signals and written train orders governed traffic on the St. Paul District. *(Roger Puta, M. Finzer collection)*

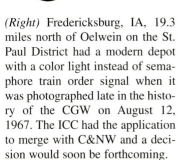 **FREDERICKSBURG**

*(Right)* Fredericksburg, IA, 19.3 miles north of Oelwein on the St. Paul District had a modern depot with a color light instead of semaphore train order signal when it was photographed late in the history of the CGW on August 12, 1967. The ICC had the application to merge with C&NW and a decision would soon be forthcoming.
*(Roger E. Puta, M. Finzer collection)*

# Des Moines & Kansas City Districts

Extending over the 252.9 miles from Oelwein to Kansas City Union Station, these two districts of the Eastern division formed the line into Kansas City, one of four major terminals of the Chicago Great Western. From Leavenworth, KS into Kansas City, 26.7 miles, trackage rights over the Missouri Pacific were exercised. CGW owned the bridge over the Missouri River at Leavenworth. Waterloo, Des Moines and St. Joseph were the most important originators and terminators of tonnage between Oelwein and Kansas City. Meat packing houses in Waterloo, also farm machinery manufacturers furnished considerable tonnage to CGW. Packing house products moving from St. Joseph moved east mostly on Burlington and the Santa Fe, however CGW got some by-products, and also considerable grain products billed from St. Joseph. Other stations between Oelwein and Kansas City were of negligible importance, however before trucks took over the hauling of livestock, hogs and cattle were loaded at many points, also grain from country elevators. Automatic block signals were in service between Marshalltown and Diagonal. For most of the route, the speed limit for freight trains was 45 m.p.h. and for passenger trains 60 m.p.h. with 55 m.p.h. between Diagonal and Leavenworth. Missouri Pacific had centralized traffic control over the portion the CGW used, into the Ohio Avenue, Kansas City freight yard. During the Deramus-Reidy eras, passenger train service was limited to Nos. 5-6, the former MILL CITIES LIMITED, until its discontinuance on April 27, 1962. Regular southbound manifest freight trains were Nos. 41 and 43, with Nos. 92 and 42 operated northbound. By the 1960s, No. 43 was frequently annulled, with an extra operated on days of heavy traffic. No. 42 was usually the only northbound through freight, leaving Kansas City in the evening. Yard engines were assigned at Waterloo, Des Moines, St. Joseph and Kansas City.

## FAIRBANK

*(Above)* Manifest train 41 passed the depot at Fairbank, IA, 7.4 miles from Oelwein on the afternoon of October 18, 1952. F3A 113C and three companions were rolling 113 cars to Des Moines, St. Joseph and Kansas City. *(W.L. Heitter)*

 # WATERLOO

*(Left)* Attractively painted 101C, which left EMD in October 1947 as the second CGW F3A was ready to couple to an outbound train at Waterloo on January 2, 1953. *(D.E. Lodge)*

| Capacity of Other Tracks, Locations of Water and Fuel Stations, Turntables, Track Scales, Wyes. | Capacity of Sidings. | Distance from St. Paul. | | TIME TABLE No. 10 Effective March 2, 1958 | NORTHBOUND | | |
|---|---|---|---|---|---|---|---|
| | | | | | FIRST CLASS | SECOND CLASS | |
| | | | | | 6 Passenger | 42 Manifest Freight | 92 Manifest Freight |
| | | | | | Arrive Daily Ex. Sunday | Arrive Daily | Arrive Daily |
| Yard-W-O-S-Y | | 178.5 | PH-R-Ry | OELWEIN | 10.15AM | 1.00PM | 1.40AM |
| | | | | 7.4 | | 41 | |
| 21 | 180 | 185.9 | PH | FAIRBANK | f 10.00 | 12.30PM | 1.15 |
| | | | | 7.7 | | | |
| 17 | | 193.6 | PH | DUNKERTON | f 9.45 | | |
| | | | | 10.8 | | | |
| Yard-W-O-S Conn. Interlocked | 128 | 204.4 | PH-R | WATERLOO | s 9.30 | 11.45AM | 12.25AM |
| | | | | I. C. R. R. Crossing 0.5 | | | |
| Auto. Signals | | 204.9 | | C. R. I. & P. Crossing | | | |
| | | | | 5.7 | | | |
| 11 | 20-S | 210.6 | PH | CEDAR FALLS JCT. | 8.50 | | |
| | | | | 3.3 | | | |
| 45 | 80 | 213.9 | PH | HUDSON | s 8.45 | 10.50 | 11.10PM |
| Auto. Signals | | 218.8 | | C. & N. W. Crossing | | | 43 |
| | | | | 4.4 | | | |
| Connection 22 Auto. Signals | | 223.2 | PH. { | REINBECK C. R. I. & P. Crossing } | s 8.30 | | |
| | | | | 7.1 | | | |
| 25 | 108 | 230.3 | PH | LINCOLN | f 8.18 | 10.20 | 10.40 |
| | | | | 5.5 | | | |
| Auto. Signals S Conn. No. End | | 235.8 | PH. { | C. & N. W. Crossing GLADBROOK } | s 8.09 | 10.05 | 10.30 |
| | | | | 8.9 | | | |
| 28 | 55 | 244.7 | PH | GREEN MOUNTAIN | f 7.55 | | |
| | | | | 5.2 | | | |
| Yard | | 249.9 | | POWERVILLE | | | |
| | | | | 0.5 | | | |
| | 117 | 250.4 | PH | NORTH MARSHALLTOWN | 7.45 | 9.30 | 10.00 |
| | | | | 1.6 | | | |
| Not Gated | | 252.0 | | C. & N. W. Crossing | | | |
| | | | | 0.2 | | | |
| Yard W.O.S.Y | 141 | 252.2 | PH-R | MARSHALLTOWN | s 7.40 | 9.00 | 9.55 |
| | | | | 0.8 | | | |
| Conn. Interlocked 30 | | 253.0 | | C. & N. W.-M. & St. L. Crossings 12.8 | | | |
| | 56 | 265.8 | PH | MELBOURNE | f 7.15 | 8.25 | 9.15 |
| | | | | 9.1 | | | |
| 30 | 58 | 274.9 | PH | BAXTER | f 7.01 | | |
| | | | | 9.2 | | | |
| 22 | 50 | 284.1 | PH | MINGO | f 6.47 | 7.45 | 8.35 |
| | | | | 12.7 | | | |
| 25 | 131 | 296.8 | PH | BONDURANT | f 6.29 | 7.15 | 8.10 |
| | | | | 6.7 | | 5 | |
| 25-North | | 303.5 | PH | NORWOOD | | | |
| | | | | 1.6 | | | |
| 20 | | 305.1 | | HIGHLAND | | | |
| | | | | 2.9 | | | |
| Interlocked | | 306.0 | | C. R. I. & P. Crossing | | | |
| | | | | 0.7 | | | |
| | 39 | 306.7 | PH | REDDY | 5.55 | 6.48 | 7.40 |
| | | | | 0.1 | | 5 | |
| Connections Not Gated | | 306.8 | { | C. R. I. & P.—D. M. U. and C. B. & Q. Crossings } | | | |
| | | | | 2.1 | 43-42 | 6-43 | 41 |
| Yard-W-O-S | | 310.9 | PH-R | DES MOINES | 5.45AM | 6.00AM | 7.15PM |
| | | 132.4 | | | Depart Daily Ex. Sunday | Depart Daily | Depart Daily |
| | | | | Time on District | 4.30 | 7.00 | 6.25 |

DES MOINES DISTRICT — DES MOINES TO OELWEIN

*(Above)* On the outskirts of Waterloo F3A 101C, F3B 101D, F3B 106B, F3A 106A move manifest train 41 to Kansas City, on a sunny January 2, 1953. A photograph with a freight train that included a TOFC or "piggyback" car in 1953 was not common. *(D.E. Lodge)*

*(Right)* A side view of Baldwin Switcher 40 at Waterloo, also on January 2, 1953. CGW rostered ten DS4-4-1000 models all built in 1949. Nos. 32, 38 and 39 lasted long enough to become C&NW 1073, 1074, 1075.
*(D.E. Lodge)*

*(Above)* Baldwin DS4-4-1000 of CGW Class D-3, engine 40 was doing switching chores at Waterloo on January 2, 1953 as a set of Fs headed by F3A 106A was making a pick up. 106A was not retired until February 1970, almost two years after the CGW-C&NW merger. *(D.E. Lodge)*

*(Below)* NW2 16 was a regular yard switcher at Waterloo during the last years of independent CGW operation. On March 11, 1967, the nineteen-year-old was on the tie-up track.

*(Roger E. Puta, M. Finzer collection)*

##  DES MOINES

*(Above)* "Cow-calf" TR2 60A-60B and NW-2 30 were assigned as the Des Moines Bell Avenue yard switchers in February 1959. At this time, sister 58A-58B was leased to the power short Missouri-Kansas-Texas for switching service at Parsons, KS. The 30 was the only NW2 to be renumbered by the C&NW, becoming 1016. *(R.D. Sims)*

*(Below)* Somewhat the worse for wear, NW2 22 was doing switching duty at the Des Moines Bell Avenue yard on April 22, 1963. Built in May 1948, the 1000 h.p. unit was still on the roster when the CGW merged with C&NW July 1, 1968. *(R.D. Sims)*

*(Left)* Another NW2 assigned to yard service at Des Moines was the 23, which was on hand at the engine terminal on June 30, 1963. It was one of the 14 NW2s built between April and June 1948.
*(R.D. Sims)*

*(Below)* The crew aboard NW2 #22 at Des Moines on this hot June 30, 1963 probably want to finish work with that ripe old stock car as soon as possible. F3A 101A and five other Fs wait for an outbound call on an adjacent track. *(R.D. Sims)*

*(Above)* The 9000 h.p. set of F units on hand at Des Moines on June 30, 1963, included 101A-102B-106D-105D-115D-109A. 105D-106D-115D were F7Bs built in 1949-1950 as CGW expanded its freight engine consists beyond the normal four-unit 6000 h.p. set-ups. The other early F3s were among the first sold to a U.S. railroad in the fall of 1947, for freight service. *(R.D. Sims)*

*(Below)* A comparison of the two CGW "covered wagon" paint schemes on January 7, 1968, at the Des Moines engine terminal. 106A built in October 1947, and 108A, which followed in March 1948 were fast approaching the end of their economic lives. The 106A has the more elderly look of the tall roof fan housings, which were discontinued after 1947. *(R.D. Sims)*

 **ST. JOSEPH**

*(Above)* A four-car No. 5, behind F7A #154 was passing through St. Joseph enroute from Minneapolis to Kansas City on a morning in June 1960. Slightly less than two years later, the last CGW passenger train would stop at "Saint Joe." *(Emery J. Gulash)*

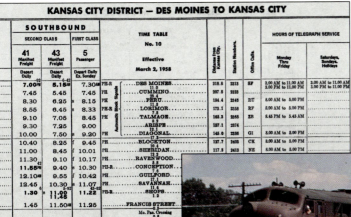

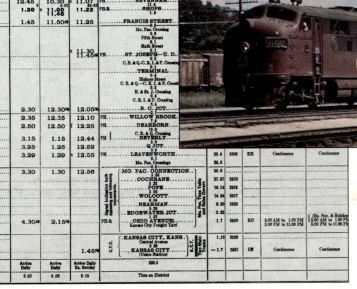

*(Above)* A four-unit consist of Fs, controlled by F3A 110C passed through St. Joseph on July 16, 1963. Freight train crews were running through between Des Moines and Kansas City, 217 miles, a long crew district in the 1960s. *(Charly's slides)*

# Kansas City

With connections to eleven Class I railroads, plus the Kansas City Terminal Railway, Kansas City was one of four principal Chicago Great Western terminals from its entry in 1891 until merger in 1968. Trackage rights over the Missouri Pacific offered a water level grade to Leavenworth, permitting 2-8-2 type steam locomotives to handle 4000 tons. At Kirmeyer, on the east side of the Missouri River, 2-10-4 type power handled 3500 tons on prevailing one percent grades to Des Moines. As the last railroad to enter Kansas City, CGW served few on-line industries, but reciprocal switching arrangements with the other railroads allowed Great Western access to and from the many shippers in the Kansas City switching district. Freight operations were centered at the Ohio Avenue yard, located near where the Kansas River flowed into the Missouri River. Severe flooding occurred in this area during the summer of 1951. With its restricted area, the Ohio Avenue yard could not be expanded for the longer trains that dieselization brought beginning in 1947-1948, and it was a common practice, to "double" trains over after arrivals and before departures. During the diesel era, manifest trains 41 at 430 a.m. and 43 at 215 p.m. were daily arrivals with 92 at 830 a.m. and 42 at 700 p.m. departing. By the 1960s, on many days, only one train in each direction operated. The consist of No. 42 from Kansas City on August 13, 1963 provides information on commodities handled. On this summer day a car of grapes off Union Pacific, and a car of peaches off Santa Fe, both for Des Moines, plus one meat from the Swift & Co. plant in Kansas City moving through to Chicago, were the only perishable loads. Other freight included six flour and feed, five household goods, 18 oil and other petroleum products, six chemicals, three steel, three paper, six rubber, five phosphate rock and seven other single loads of other commodities. Cars received off other railroads included 20 from Kansas City Southern, nine from Santa Fe, 12 from Frisco, 14 from Missouri Pacific, four from Katy and single cars from Rock Island, Union Pacific and Wabash. No cars came from the Milwaukee, Burlington or Gulf, Mobile & Ohio. The balance of train 42 originated in Kansas City. In 1963, the CGW was a vital part of the nation's railway network. During the passenger train era, CGW used the Kansas City Union Station from 1914 until the April 27, 1962 discontinuance of Kansas City-Minneapolis Trains Nos. 5-6.

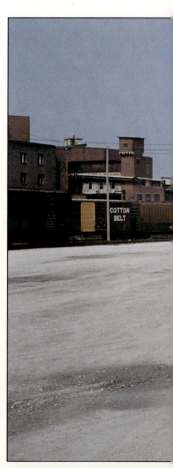

*(Above)* TR2 60A-60B was enroute over Santa Fe trackage, near the Kansas River, east of the AT&SF Argentine yard with a transfer to the Ohio Avenue yard in April 1966. Transfer caboose 180 trails the 1949 built "cow-calf."
*(D.O. Rush)*

*(Above)* On March 26, 1967 a four-unit set of GP30s had arrived at the Ohio Avenue yard on morning train No. 41. Engine and train crews found the 2250 h.p. "Geeps" to be welcome successors to the veteran Fs. They were much appreciated on trains that did any pick-up or set-out work enroute due to better visibility and quicker starts. *(Bill Volkmer collection)*

*(Below)* A view from the east end of the Ohio Avenue yard in June 1967, with crimson painted "covered wagons" on hand. A small TOFC or "piggyback" facility was maintained at Ohio Avenue for Kansas City customers. *(D.O. Rush)*

*(Above)* F3A 107C headed up a consist of F units laying over at the Ohio Avenue yard in Kansas City in June 1967. The 107C was built by EMD in March 1948 and worked briefly on the Chicago & North Western as number 203. *(D.O. Rush)*

*(Left)* "Eastern style" cupola caboose 607, built in 1946 and newer baywindow 625, a 1955 product of International Car Company were on the Ohio Avenue caboose track in June 1967. 607 would become C&NW 10506 and 625 would be re-numbered C&NW 10524, both in November 1972. *(D.O. Rush)*

*(Below)* TR2 58 assigned to Kansas City transfer service was on the engine service track at the Ohio Avenue yard in June 1967. Diesel fuel storage tanks are at the left and the sanding tower at the right of this photo. *(D.O. Rush)*

*(Above)* Another view in June 1967 of the Ohio Avenue CGW facility in Kansas City. The advertising signs in the background are for motorists using the busy Intercity Viaduct between Kansas City, MO and Kansas City, KS. In the steam era, the small roundhouse and its visitors could easily be observed off the viaduct. *(D.O. Rush)*

*(Below)* The Deramus era freight office and older freight house on the south side of the Ohio Avenue yard in June 1967. CGW had exited the less than carload business by that date, but the office was still used by the local agent and other operating personnel. *(D.O. Rush)*

*(Above)* An August day in 1967 saw half of the eight CGW GP30s on hand at the Ohio Avenue yard waiting for the evening departure of manifest freight train No. 42 to Oelwein, 383.5 mostly hilly miles away. *(D.O. Rush)*

*(Below)* A TR2 powered transfer prepares to leave the Ohio Avenue yard in August 1967, as a Frisco Baldwin switcher arrives with cars for the CGW. *(D.O. Rush)*

*(Above)* On April 7, 1966, train 91 headed into the sunset at Dubuque (Wood), Iowa, detouring on the Illinois Central. In two more years the entire railroad would approach its final sunset as on July 1, 1968, the Chicago Great Western would be absorbed by the Chicago & North Western. It is only fitting that our final photo should typify the Great Western we fondly recall. *(Mike Nelson)*